Contents

Preface

This research project arose in 1983 from the clear need to provide objective information on the status of fish in Scottish lochs in relation to acid deposition. It was already known at that time that fish had disappeared from several lochs in one part of the country (Galloway), and that these lochs had become more acid during the last few decades. However, it was not known how widespread this phenomenon was across the country as a whole, and the main objective of the study was to examine this question on as broad a basis as possible, within the timescale of the contract involved (2.5 years).

This report on the study is divided into 3 main parts, each of which is self-contained.

1. A brief summary of the main objectives, methods, results and conclusions of the study.

2. A general account of the work, including the principal results, conclusions and suggestions for future research.

3. A series of 5 appendices giving scientific accounts of each part of the project and details of the main results in relation to loch bathymetry and hydrology, water chemistry, fish in lochs, fish in streams, and tail deformities in fish.

Natural Environment Research Council

Acidification and fish in Scottish lochs

P S MAITLAND, A A LYLE and R N B CAMPBELL

INSTITUTE OF TERRESTRIAL ECOLOGY

Printed in Great Britain by
Cambrian News (Aberystwyth) Ltd
© NERC Copyright 1987

Published in 1987 by
Institute of Terrestrial Ecology
Merlewood Research Station
GRANGE-OVER-SANDS
Cumbria LA11 6JU

BRITISH LIBRARY CATALOGUING-IN-PUBLICATION DATA
Acidification and fish in Scottish lochs   1. Fish populations—Scotland. 2. Acidification—
Scotland. 3 Fishes—Scotland—Effect of water pollution
I. Maitland, P.S. II.Lyle, A.A. III. Campbell, R.N.B.
597'.05248'09411   QL618.3
   ISBN 1 870393 04 X

COVER ILLUSTRATION
A catch of brown trout, the common fish of Scotland's hill lochs, taken from the Round Loch of
the Dungeon in Galloway in October 1984 (Photograph R N B Campbell)

ACKNOWLEDGEMENTS

This project was funded under contract by the Commission of the European Communities and
the UK Department of the Environment.

We are grateful to a number of colleagues who took part in the field work and helped in other
ways: S M Adair, K East, D H Jones, L May, K H Morris, I R Smith and T Varley. Much of the map
work was done by P H Hutchinson but assistance with various aspects was given by C Watt, M
Munro, R I Smith, R W Battarbee and J Pytches. All chemical analyses were carried out by the
ITE Chemical Services Section and we thank S E Allen and J D Roberts and his staff for all their
advice and help. A Booth made many useful comments on the text and P Ward gave invaluable
help in preparing the text for publication.

Permission to visit sites was normally freely given by owners and in several cases help with
transport and other matters was also given. We would like to acknowledge the following:
Ardtalla Estates (Mr J A MacTaggart); Ardtornish Estate (Mr A F G Robertson); Mrs Baird;
Balmoral Estate (Mr M R M Leslie); Mr I J Bennett; Black Mount Estate (Mr G Fleming);
Cairndow Estate (Mrs Bennett, Mr G Cameron); Callumkill Estate (Mr J G Macgoun); Mr D F
Culham; Dunecht Estates (Mr I R Douglas); Dunlossit Estates (Maj McKay-Forbes); Forestry
Commission (Mr E J S Michie, Mr C Bancroft, Mr W Norrie); Forrest Estate (Mr R Watson); Lt
Col J B F Fortune; Fountain Forestry (Mr E F Bell, Mr R MacNicol, Mr W Lyon); Mr J Gilroy;
Glenfernas Estate (Lord Leven); Grampian Regional Council (Mr I D Brown); Laggan Estates (Mr
F D Morison, Mr D Fraser); Leorin Estates (Mr Speltham); Lochendorb Estate (Mr Laing);
National Trust for Scotland; Mrs H Paterson; Rothiemurchus Estates (Mr J Grant); Shurreray
Estate (Sir D Black, Mr W Crothers); Mrs P Strutt.

The *Institute of Terrestrial Ecology (ITE)* was established in 1973, from the former Nature
Conservancy's research stations and staff, joined later by the Institute of Tree Biology and the
Culture Centre of Algae and Protozoa. ITE contributes to, and draws upon, the collective
knowledge of the 14 sister institutes which make up the *Natural Environment Research Council*
spanning all the environmental sciences.

The Institute studies the factors determining the structure, composition and processes of land
and freshwater systems, and of individual plant and animal species. It is developing a sounder
scientific basis for predicting and modelling environmental trends arising from natural or
man-made change. The results of this research are available to those responsible for the
protection, management and wise use of our natural resources.

One quarter of ITE's work is research commissioned by customers, such as the Department of
Environment, the Commission of the European Communities, the Nature Conservancy Council
and the Overseas Development Administration. The remainder is fundamental research
supported by NERC.

ITE's expertise is widely used by international organizations in overseas projects and
programmes of research.

Dr P S Maitland
Institute of Terrestrial Ecology
Bush Estate
Penicuik, Midlothian
EH26 0QB
Scotland

031 445 4343

Summary

1. Fish populations in waters in Scandinavia and other parts of the northern hemisphere have been seriously affected in recent years by acidification from atmospheric pollutants. The objective of this study was to determine to what extent waters in Scotland may have been affected in the same way.

2. From the literature and data from waters in Galloway, it was evident that lochs lying on granitic bedrock are more vulnerable to acidification than most others, so the study concentrated on this type of water. The numbers and distribution of lochs on granite throughout the country were determined from maps. A total of 1536 lochs was recorded; 377 of them had a surface area greater than one hectare, and 279 of these had catchments entirely on granite.

3. A list of lochs was prepared for field survey, which included not only lochs whose catchments lay entirely on granite, but also a series of 'control' lochs which lay entirely outwith granite. During 1984 and 1985, 83 lochs were visited in various parts of Scotland. At each site, bathymetry and fish in the loch were studied, as well as water chemistry and fish in the inflow and outflow streams.

4. Bathymetric information was obtained for 64 lochs. Their theoretical retention times varied from 1.2 hours to 4.25 years. These and other physical data were examined for the possible influence of basic hydrological factors on loch acidification. Two aspects were felt to be important: first, the relative amounts of direct and catchment-affected rain entering a loch, and, second, the influence exercised by throughflow.

5. Chemical analyses indicated a general similarity among waters in the same geographic area but wide differences between some geographic areas. A number of sites was shown to be chemically acidified, the majority being in Galloway.

6. In Galloway, there are 38 lochs on the Doon and Cairnsmore blocks, 23 of which are more than one ha in area. Eleven of these larger lochs were studied: all were found to be acidified chemically and 6 were fishless. Over the rest of Scotland there are 354 lochs greater than 1 hectare lying on granite: 38 of these were examined but most showed no signs of acidification and only 4 were fishless.

7. Many of the Galloway lochs, previously known to hold fish populations, are now fishless. Trout populations in other lochs categorized as acidified on chemical criteria had population characteristics such as low numbers, increased individual size and condition and faster growth, consistent with the effect of increasing acidification.

8. An unknown factor encountered in this research was the effect of acidification on the brown, organically stained waters so common in Scotland. There is little information on the impact of acid deposition on such waters but it is possible that inorganic aluminium toxicity cannot occur in waters containing more than certain levels of organic material.

9. Seven different fish species were found in the inflow and outflow streams of the 63 lochs where electro-fishing was carried out. Thirty-three per cent of the inflows and 32% of the outflows were apparently fishless and most of these were categorized as being acidified chemically. Virtually all the control streams contained fish.

10. Old records of tail deformities in brown trout proved to be from lochs which are now acidified and fishless. Tail deformities were found in fish from several of the other study lochs, all of which were shown to be chemically acidified.

11. The broad conclusion from this study is that acidification has affected a number of waters in Scotland and rendered some of them fishless. The great majority of these are in Galloway. Waters in other, potentially vulnerable, areas are much less affected, possibly due to the ameliorating effect of soils, particularly peat in many places.

The status of fish populations in waters likely to have been affected by acid deposition in Scotland

P S MAITLAND, A A LYLE and R N B CAMPBELL

1 Introduction

Although known to be a problem since the 1920s, it is only over the last 15 years or so that ecologists in the northern hemisphere have become increasingly concerned about the impact of acid deposition on freshwater ecosystems and other parts of the environment (Almer 1974; Beamish et al. 1975; Harvey 1975; Haines 1981). In Scandinavia (especially southern Sweden and Norway), and more recently in North America (both in Canada and the USA), numerous scientific studies related to the problem have been initiated and there has been a massive growth in the literature over the last few years. Many other countries are now involved in work on acid deposition, but in Great Britain the input in the field of freshwater ecology has been relatively small until recently (United Kingdom Acid Waters Review Group 1986).

Considerable general agreement appears to be developing from the research data (involving field survey, monitoring and experimental work) produced in Scandinavia and North America (Drablos & Tollan 1980; Haines 1981; Johnson 1982). Rain in many parts of the world—including the British Isles (United Kingdom Review Group on Acid Rain 1983; Mathews et al. 1984)—is acid and has probably become more so during this century. This rain and associated dry deposition appear to have acidified some fresh waters—especially those in areas of base-poor geology whose buffering capacity is low.

Organisms at each major trophic level are affected by this acidification. The diversity of phytoplankton decreases with acidification but the production of some algae and mosses increases (Battarbee 1984). The diversity and production of most macrophyte communities decrease with decreasing pH, and the same appears to be true of zooplankton and zoobenthos, though the situation is more complex with invertebrates (Engblom & Lingdell 1983). If the acidification is sufficiently great to exclude fish, then their absence as the normal top predators can lead to an unusual abundance of some prey species. Amphibians (Tome & Pough 1982) and birds (Eriksson 1984) can also be affected.

One of the earliest indicators of acid pollution and one of its most important effects was the disappearance of many fish—especially salmonids (Atlantic salmon *Salmo salar*, brown trout *Salmo trutta* and arctic charr *Salvelinus alpinus*)—from rivers and lakes in which they were previously abundant (Wright & Snekvic 1978; Muniz & Leivestad 1980; Harvey & Lee 1982; Schofield 1982). For example, Atlantic salmon have disappeared from many rivers in southern Scandinavia and the number of lakes in these areas without populations of brown trout and arctic charr has increased dramatically, especially over the last 15 years (Overrein et al. 1980; Johnson 1982). Massive kills of salmon and trout have been observed during snowmelt and after heavy rain (Henriksen et al. 1984).

Only recently has any significant interest been taken in the effect of acid deposition on fresh waters in Great Britain (Watt Committee on Energy 1984; United Kingdom Acid Waters Review Group 1986), although the Scandinavians have long felt that Britain is one of the important sources of the excess atmospheric acidity affecting their fresh waters. Moreover, the approach to research has been complicated by the fact that (i) there are few background data of sufficient antiquity from appropriate waters with which the current situation can be compared, (ii) there is a complex interaction between the atmosphere, coniferous forests (whose area in Great Britain, especially Scotland, has increased enormously over the last few decades) and acid input to adjacent streams, and (iii) many upland waters are brown and organically stained.

Thus, there is no doubt that acid deposition is having a significant and increasing impact on fresh waters in extensive areas of Scandinavia, North America and elsewhere (Wright et al. 1980). It is highly likely that similar changes are taking place in some fresh waters in Great Britain where the rain is acid (Cape et al. 1984) and the underlying rocks have a low buffering capacity (Harriman & Wells 1985). However, until very recently, most research in Britain had been peripheral to the problem, and little of it directly answered the question of whether fresh waters in Great Britain have been extensively affected by acid deposition.

The most relevant work at the start of the present project was that carried out in Galloway and the Loch Ard area of Scotland by Harriman and Morrison (1980, 1981, 1982). Some work has also been carried out in Wales (Stoner et al. 1984). Recently, many other relevant projects have started in different parts of the United Kingdom with a variety of objectives. The most relevant study of all to the present work was the background survey of water chemistry carried out in 1979 in south-west Scotland (from Norway) by Wright and Henriksen (1980).

The present project is primarily a study of the fish populations of selected waters in adjacent granite and non-granite areas likely to be affected by acid precipitation. The main objective has been to reveal how many waters are fishless and to compare existing with previous data for these waters. The latter are mainly angling records which, though never quantitative and sometimes anecdotal, are adequate as far as presence/absence comparisons are concerned.

The objectives of the present project were as follows.

i.   To select, by means of a desk study of topographical, geological and atmospheric deposition maps, suitable sets of study lochs in adjacent granite and non-granite areas of Scotland. The catchments of these lochs were subsequently classified according to land use.

ii.   Where possible, to gather information on the historical status of the fish populations of these waters from the published literature, estate records, anglers and others.

iii.   To sample the fish populations in the lochs, their inflows and outflows using conventional fishery methods and to ascertain background water chemistry, bathymetry and hydrology.

2 Desk study: lochs on granite
The total number of lochs in Scotland, in various size, and other, categories, has been determined by Smith and Lyle (1979). The assumption in the present study is that those lochs lying on granite bedrock are among the most vulnerable to acid deposition; a necessary preliminary to any field work was to determine the numbers and distribution of such lochs. From this information it would then be possible to select suitable sets of waters, including controls, for study.

2.1 Map survey
The main objectives of the desk study, therefore, were to transfer the boundaries of the granite areas of Scotland from geological survey maps to 1:50000 scale Ordnance Survey (OS) topographical maps, and to determine the number of lochs of various size classes within these areas.

The granite areas of Scotland were traced from the British Geological Survey collection of geological maps at either 1:63360 or 1:50000 scales, with the exception of 5 maps which were unavailable. The collection of geological maps consisted of solid, solid and drift and drift editions. The granite areas on any given geological map were traced on to one sheet of tracing paper, together with grid line reference marks. Intrusions of non-granitic rock within the granite blocks were also marked.

The transfer of information at the 1:50000 scale was a simple matter but where the geological maps were at a scale of 1:63360, other methods were used. (1) The appropriate 1:63360 scale OS map was overlaid with the tracing and the information transferred to the 1:50000 scale OS maps by eye, using grid lines and cartographic features for reference. (2) The tracings were photographically enlarged to a 1:50000 scale. Grid lines enabled identification of any distortion, but with care this was negligible. The latter method enabled a more rapid and accurate transfer of the solid geology to the OS maps. In some cases, the tracings had to be taken from hand-painted geological maps where the absence of grid lines meant that distortion could only be detected by reference to the appropriate 1:63360 and 1:625000 geological maps.

In 3 cases, the outlines of the granite areas bore little resemblance to the 1:625000 geological map. The areas covered by these sheets were, therefore, tranferred by grid overlay from the 1:625000 geological map. Similarly, those areas not covered by geological maps at either 1:63360 or 1:50000 scale were drawn in from the 1:625000 scale map using a grid overlay.

Having transferred the granite areas to the 1:50000 scale maps, a method of identifying the granite blocks within the 5 major geological areas of Scotland was devised by modification of the block nomenclature system of Anderson (1939). Thus, within the 5 regions of Scotland (viz north-west Highlands, northern Highlands, Grampian Highlands, midland valley and southern uplands), each granite block was given a number and name (see Figure 1 & Table 1). The only exceptions to this system were the Shetlands and Outer Hebrides, which were treated separately.

2.2 Loch counts
Using the system of granite block nomenclature outlined above, a count was made of all lochs whose basins were located entirely within areas of granite. The lochs were allocated to 8 size classes (<1, 1-4, 4-12.5, 12.5-25, 25-50, 50-100, 100-200 and >200 ha) by using grid overlays to determine the surface area, and any named lochs were noted. This procedure was followed for each granite block and the data were recorded on regional data sheets. A master sheet, which incorporated the data from all the regions, was then constructed (Table 2). Details of lochs whose basins occurred partially within granite blocks were recorded as footnotes on the regional data sheets.

Because the study was concerned with the status of fish in areas likely to have been affected by acid deposition, and as lochs whose basins are within granite may have catchments predominantly outwith granite areas, it was decided to make a further count of 'pure granite' lochs. Thus, all lochs >1 ha in surface area whose catchments were located entirely within the granite blocks were counted using the same procedure as above. A new master sheet was then produced from these data (Table 3). The effect of imposing this new standard was to shift the location of potential sites for field sampling towards the centres of the granite blocks. In many instances, the younger, more acidic granites are located near the middle of the

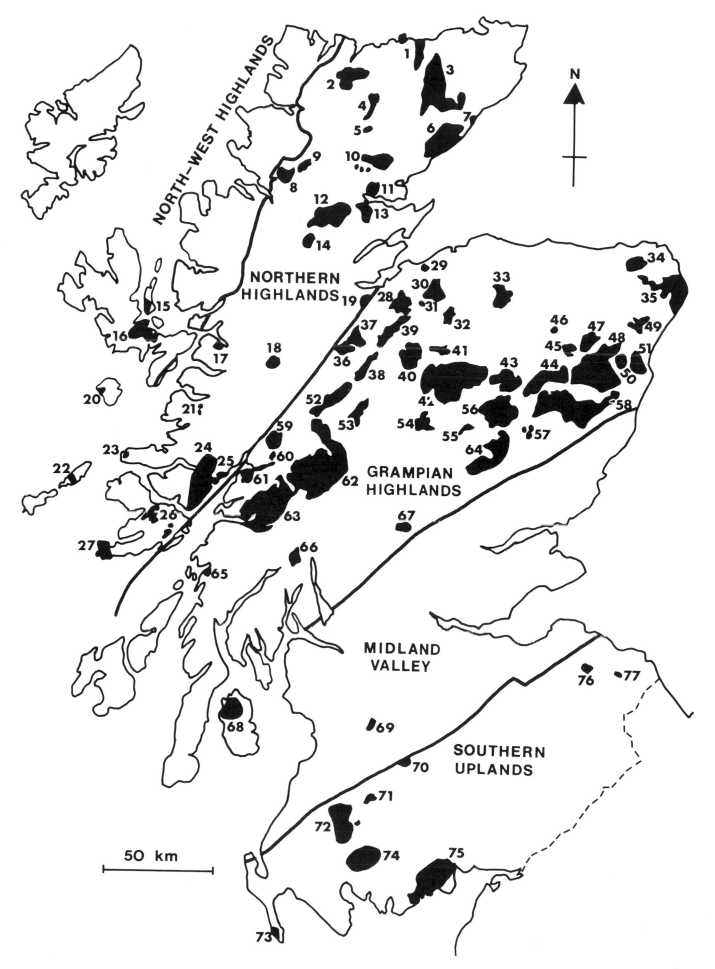

Figure 1. The principal granite blocks in Scotland, modified from Anderson (1939)

Table 1. The system of naming the granite blocks of Scotland

Number	Name	Number	Name
1	Strathy & Strath Halladale	40	Monadhliath
2	Loch Loyal	41	Boat of Garten
3	Caithness	42	Cairngorm
4	Strathnaver	43	Glen Cairn
5	Loch Gaineamhach	44	Ballater
6	Helmsdale	45	Alford
7	Newport	46	Cairn More
8	Loch Borralan	47	Bennachie
9	Ben More	48	Hill of Fare
10	Lairg (& satellite blocks)	49	Pitmedden
11	Migdale	50	Kinellar
12	Kildermorie Forest	51	Aberdeen
13	Fearn	52	Corrieyairack
14	Strath Rannoch	53	Dalwhinnie
15	Raasay	54	Beinn Dearg
16	Skye	55	Carn Mor
17	Loch Duich	56	Lochnagar
18	Cluanie	57	Ben Tirran Group
19	Loch Ness (north)	58	Mount Battock
20	Rhum	59	Ben Nevis
21	South Morar	60	Mullach Nan Coirean
22	Coll	61	Ballachullish
23	Ardnamurchan	62	Moor of Rannoch
24	Morvern-Strontian	63	Etive complex
25	Loch Linnhe	64	Caenlochan
26	Mull	65	Loch Melfort
27	Ross of Mull	66	Glen Fyne
28	Moy	67	Glen Lednock
29	Nairn	68	Arran
30	Ardclach	69	Distinkhorn
31	Loch Winter	70	Lowther Hills
32	Grantown on Spey	71	Cairnsmore/Carsphairn
33	Benn Rinnes	72	Loch Doon
34	Strichen	73	Mull of Galloway
35	Peterhead	74	Cairnsmore/Fleet
36	Knockie Lodge	75	Criffel
37	Foyers	76	Lammermuirs (N)
38	Sherramore Forest	77	Lammermuirs (S)
39	Tomatin		

nature were noted separately and termed 'fringe' lochs.

From the data now available, it was possible to prepare a list of potential sites for study in the field. For all 'pure' lochs >1 ha within the granite blocks under consideration, various catchment details, such as size class, altitude, number of inflows, presence of outflows, degree of catchment afforestation, method and ease of access, were recorded. During site selection, lochs with neither an inflow nor an outflow were not normally considered, as it was felt that these lochs would be unlikely to be able to support natural trout populations anyway, given their requirement for running water at spawning time. The names given on the 1:50000 OS maps were those used for the lochs. Where no name was given to a loch, a 'name' was allocated from the nearest named cartographic feature—usually a topographical one.

'Control' lochs were also selected from the 1:50000 OS maps. They were chosen for their proximity to granite blocks but their catchments were entirely outwith granite. Where possible, the control sites were of a similar size and had catchment characteristics resembling those of the study sites. At least one appropriate control loch was chosen for each granite block containing one or more study sites.

A master list of potential study sites was prepared, initially to be issued to sports fishermen. In order to avoid biased reports from anglers, study sites and control sites were not identified and it was stressed in an accompanying questionnaire that the list included lochs of varying susceptibility to acidification. About 500 of these lists and questionnaires, asking for details of past catches from any of the lochs concerned, were issued to anglers all over Scotland.

blocks (Anderson 1939), a factor which is relevant to the objectives of the study. However, for logistic reasons, the shift had serious implications for gaining access to many sites. Furthermore, because catchment size tends to increase with loch size, very few large (>100 ha) 'pure' lochs were available for study. For this reason, a small number of lochs whose catchments were predominantly (>75%) granitic in

Background information on each loch was collected from Murray and Pullar (1910) and other sources. Finally, lochs to be sampled in the field were selected. This selection was in some ways a progressive process, and ultimately the choice of lochs visited depended on various factors such as access, permission, weather, geographic distribution, features of apparent special interest, etc. A full list of all those visited is given in Table 4.

Table 2. The number of lochs in different size classes whose basins occur entirely within granite blocks

Region	<1	1-4	4-12.5	12.5-25	25-50	50-100	100-200	>200	Total
Southern uplands	30	14	10	2	3	5	2	0	66
Midland valley	47	2	2	0	1	0	0	0	52
Grampian Highlands	514	84	31	5	6	5	2	4	651
Northern Highlands	284	79	24	10	6	1	0	1	405
North-west Highlands	21	6	1	0	0	0	0	0	28
Western Isles	17	7	4	1	0	0	0	0	29
Shetland & Orkney	246	40	13	4	1	1	0	0	309
Total	1159	232	85	22	17	12	4	5	1536

Table 3. The number of lochs of >1 ha in different size classes whose catchments occur entirely within granite blocks

Region	Size class (ha) <1	1-4	4-12.5	12.5-25	25-50	50-100	100-200	>200	Total
Southern uplands	—	8	7	2	1	1	1	0	20
Midland valley	—	2	2	0	1	0	0	0	5
Grampian Highlands	—	69	24	2	4	1	0	0	100
Northern Highlands	—	67	21	8	4	0	0	0	100
North-west Highlands	—	6	0	0	0	0	0	0	6
Western Isles	—	0	0	0	0	0	0	0	0
Shetland & Orkney	—	35	10	2	1	0	0	0	48
Total	—	187	64	14	11	2	1	0	279

3 Loch catchments

Once lochs had been selected for study in the field, special attention was given to the nature of the catchment of each in order to help in the understanding of its ecology, and eventually as an aid to identifying the factors most involved in the acidification process (Henriksen 1982; Bobee & Lachance 1984).

3.1 Catchment areas

The topographical catchment area of each site was identified from, and drawn on to, either 1:50000, 1:25000 or 1:10000 scale OS maps, depending on its size and difficulty of delineation. The area was then measured by planimetry. Transparent overlays of each catchment watershed were produced photographical-

Table 4. Checklist of lochs visited during the survey

Number	Loch name	NGR	Status
1	Grannoch	25542700	G
2	Fleet	25560699	G
3	Lochenbreck	25643656	C
4	am Fhaing	17687488	G
5	nan Craobh	17775484	G
6	Tearnait	17748469	G
7	Dubha 'Morvern'	17704529	C
8	Caol	17817482	G
9	Uisge	17805550	G
10	Mhic Pheadair Ruadh	27282475	C
11	Dubh 'Kingshouse W'	27273538	G
12	Dubh 'Kingshouse N'	27279541	G
13	Dubh 'Kingshouse E'	27281535	G
14	Mathair Eite	27289543	G
15	Gaineamhach	27303535	G
16	Gaineamhach 'NE'	27308538	G
17	Gaineamhach 'SE'	27311534	G
18	Einich	27913990	G*
19	Beanaidh	28911027	G
20	Mhic Ghille-chaoil	28922025	G
21	Pityoulish	28920135	C
22	na Seilge	29922587	C
23	Talaheel	29955488	G
24	nan Clach Geala	29935495	G
25	Dubh Cul Na Beinne	29984544	G
26	Tuim Ghlais	29978525	G
27	Long L of the Dungeon	25468842	G
28	Round L of the Dungeon	25467847	G
29	Enoch	25446851	G*
30	Arron	25443838	G
31	Neldricken	25445829	G*
32	Dungeon	25525845	C
33	Narroch	25452815	G
34	Round L of Glenhead	25450804	G
35	Long L of Glenhead	25446808	G
36	Valley	25445817	G
37	Harrow	25528867	C
38	Dow	25457808	G
39	Dalbeattie Plantain	25425602	G
40	Fern	25645625	G
41	White	25655547	G*
42	Barean	25615556	G
43	Clonyard	25575555	G
44	Fellcroft	25585506	C
45	Bengairn	25885522	G
46	Duff's	25425602	G
47	Kernsary	18882802	C
48	Ghiuragarstidh	18890812	C
49	Policies	38755075	G
50	Waterton	38758087	G
51	of Skene	38785075	G*
52	Brandy	38340754	C
53	Corby	38924144	C
54	Muick	38290830	G*
55	Dubh 'Muick'	37239827	G
56	Buidhe	37253827	G
57	Lochnagar	37253860	G
58	nan Eun	37230854	G
59	Sandy	37227865	G
60	Bharradail	16393634	C
61	Beinn Uraraidh	16401534	C
62	nam Breac	16408558	C
63	nam Manaichean	16398557	C
64	Laoim	16376489	C
65	Sholum	16400491	C
66	Sholum 'W'	16393489	C
67	Leorin 'W'	16368484	C
68	Leorin 'E'	16373486	C
69	na Beinne Brice	16383483	C
70	'Moine na Surdaig'	16383493	C
71	Coirre Fhionn	16901459	G
72	Iorsa	16915380	G
73	Garbad	16019238	C
74	Cnoc an Loch	16935286	G
75	a'Mhuillin	16940496	G
76	Kirkaldy	28963417	G
77	a'Chaoruinn	28755375	G
78	an t'Sidhein	28973323	C
79	nan Stuirteag	38002320	G
80	a'Mhill Bhig	27225132	C
81	a'Mhill Bhig 'Lower'	27226134	C
82	Maol Meadhonach 'Upper'	27239153	G
83	Maol Meadhonach 'Lower'	27238150	G

G = granite (G* = fringe group)
C = control

Table 5. Percentage occurrence in the catchment of major components relevant to acidification

Number	Loch name	Bedrock granite	Granite-derived drift	Soils peat	Land use conifers
1	Grannoch	100	85	28	60
2	Fleet	100	84	16	11
3	Lochenbreck	0	100	25	81
4	am Fhaing	100	100	32	0
5	nan Craobh	100	100	33	0
6	Tearnait	100	100	30	1
7	Dubha 'Morvern'	0	0	33	0
8	Caol	100	100	33	0
9	Uisge	100	82	19	0
10	Mhic Pheadair Ruadh	0	85	31	0
11	Dubh 'Kingshouse W'	100	98	31	0
12	Dubh 'Kingshouse N'	100	100	33	0
13	Dubh 'Kingshouse E'	100	100	33	0
14	Mathair Eite	100	100	33	0
15	Gaineamhach	100	100	32	0
16	Gaineamhach 'NE'	100	100	31	0
17	Gaineamhach 'SE'	100	100	33	0
18	Einich	>75	87	13	0
19	Beanaidh	100	60	20	2
20	Mhic Ghille-chaoil	100	0	50	0
21	Pityoulish	0	0	0	37
22	na Seilge	0	0	95	0
23	Talaheel	100	0	100	0
24	nan Clach Geala	100	0	100	0
25	Dubh Cul Na Beinne	100	0	100	0
26	Tuim Ghlais	100	0	100	0
27	Long L of the Dungeon	100	0	0	0
28	Round L of the Dungeon	100	67	33	10
29	Enoch	>75	90	0	0
30	Arron	100	100	0	0
31	Neldricken	>75	100	0	0
32	Dungeon	100	0	19	7
33	Narroch	100	83	17	0
34	Round L of Glenhead	100	100	0	0
35	Long L of Glenhead	100	100	0	0
36	Valley	100	96	4	0
37	Harrow	0	25	21	14
38	Dow	100	100	0	0
39	Dalbeattie Plantain	100	67	20	97
40	Fern	100	69	31	27
41	White	>75	100	0	25
42	Barean	100	100	0	66
43	Clonyard	100	100	0	7
44	Fellcroft	0	0	23	0
45	Bengairn	100	100	0	25
46	Duff's	100	100	0	64
47	Kernsary	0	0	24	5
48	Ghiuragarstidh	0	0	25	2
49	Policies	100	100	0	37
50	Waterton	100	91	12	18
51	of Skene	>75	88	8	17
52	Brandy	0	0	13	0
53	Corby	0	0	40	13
54	Muick	>75	69	34	1
55	Dubh 'Muick'	100	100	11	0
56	Buidhe	100	100	3	0
57	Lochnagar	100	100	0	0
58	nan Eun	100	100	0	0
59	Sandy	100	100	0	0
60	Bharradail	0	0	15	0
61	Beinn Uraraidh	0	0	26	0
62	nam Breac	0	0	30	0
63	nam Manaichean	0	0	25	0
64	Laoim	0	0	25	0
65	Sholum	0	0	25	0
66	Sholum 'W'	0	0	25	0
67	Leorin 'W'	0	0	25	0
68	Leorin 'E'	0	0	25	0

69	na Beinne Brice	0	0	25	0
70	'Moine na Surdaig'	0	0	25	0
71	Coirre Fhionn	100	100	15	0
72	Iorsa	100	100	25	0
73	Garbad	0	0	100	0
74	Cnoc an Loch	100	0	25	0
75	a'Mhuillin	100	31	7	0
76	Kirkaldy	100	0	63	10
77	a'Chaoruinn	100	42	67	8
78	an t'Sidhein	0	0	0	0
79	nan Stuirteag	100	0	25	0
80	a'Mhill Bhig	0	0	0	0
81	a'Mhill Bhig 'Lower'	0	0	23	0
82	Maol Meadhonach 'Upper'	100	100	0	0
83	Maol Meadhonach 'Lower'	100	100	23	0

ly, at scales to suit the soil and land use maps mentioned below.

3.2 Catchment soils
Soil maps (available at a scale of 1:250000) were used to determine the soil types present in each catchment area (Macaulay Institute 1982).In order to calculate the percentage of the catchment area covered by a particular soil type, a grid overlay was used. Square counts of each soil type within this overlay were then made to calculate the percentages for the catchment as a whole. The major soil categories involved were lithosols, alluvial soils, rankers, brown earths, podzols, surface water gleys, groundwater gleys and peats.

3.3 Catchment surface rocks
Very little quantitative information was available on the extent of exposed surface rocks in each catchment. Eventually, it was decided to make use of the information in the data books accompanying the soil maps (Macaulay Institute 1982) and to place each loch catchment area in one of the following 4 broad categories: non-rocky, moderately rocky, rocky and very rocky. This information was available from the descriptions of the drift geology of each catchment, the details of which had already been worked out as described above.

3.4 Catchment vegetation
As with rock presence, vegetation was assessed using the descriptive information supplied with the maps. The number of different categories of vegetation present was divided into the percentage of the catchment covered. The following major vegetation categories were used: moor, heath, grassland, rush pasture, bog, deciduous woodland, coniferous woodland and arable crops.

A separate analysis of land use within each catchment was made using the 1:50000 OS series. The quadrat square count method was again used and the percentage presence of each of the following categories was obtained: rough pasture, arable farmland, forest, open water and urban areas.

Data concerning some of the major relevant components from this analysis are given in Table 5.

4 Field research programme

4.1 General
The majority of the lochs concerned are in mountainous areas, often at some distance from the nearest vehicle access. This fact led to a number of logistic problems and forced a choice of equipment which was as light and portable as possible (Plate 1). Normally, a team of 4 people was required for each field trip and site visits involved walks of up to 20 km each day. Each site was visited at least twice during each trip.

4.2 Bathymetry and echo sounding surveys
Although the main focus of investigation was the fish population, it was also considered relevant to have background physical (and chemical) information for each site. At most sites, therefore, brief bathymetric surveys were made if such data were not already available (eg from Murray & Pullar 1910). It was thereafter possible to calculate loch volumes and to produce estimates of theoretical water retention times from catchment and climatic data. Water retention time is an important hydrological parameter and its potential value in the acidification context is that it allows a differentiation among sites concerning the impact of periodic inputs, from a purely hydrological aspect, which may be helpful in identifying sites at risk.

The echo surveys were made from small boats (either fibreglass or inflatable) which were dragged or carried to the lochs. A compact, portable echo sounder and battery pack were fitted to a rucksack frame and also carried to the sites. A full description of the methods and results of the bathymetric surveys is given in Appendix 1. In total, bathymetric information was obtained from surveys of 49 lochs, and equivalent data were available from 15 additional sites, mostly from Murray and Pullar (1910), making a total of 64 sites.

An additional purpose of the echo surveys was to supplement the fish catch data, with further information on fish numbers and distribution from echo traces. Overall, however, this proved unsuccessful for 2 reasons. First, many of the lochs were too shallow (<3 m) for the practical detection of fish, partly due to the narrow area sounded at these depths and partly to probable fish avoidance of the boat. Second, at a number of sites regarded as fishless or having very low stocks, dense echoes were recorded in mid-water from sources as yet unidentified. This caused uncertainty as it was not possible, with the equipment used, to make a positive distinction between echoes from fish and these other echoes. Consequently, systematic attempts to detect fish were abandoned.

4.3 Water chemistry

Sub-surface water samples were taken routinely from the major inflow to each loch and from its outflow. Where there were no inflows, or these were not running, substitute samples were taken from the loch near the point deemed most likely to have an inflow during wet weather or at the part furthest from the outflow.

Two sets of samples were always taken: one during the first visit and another during the second (usually one, 2 or 3 days later). The samples were kept in cool, dark containers until they were analysed. The range of analyses carried out included Hazen clour, pH, conductivity, calcium, magnesium, total aluminium, PO_4 phosphorus, NO_3 nitrogen, NH_4 nitrogen, chloride and SO_4 sulphur; foremost among the determinands measured were pH and calcium (Brown 1982).

4.4 Benthic invertebrates

During 1984, collections of leeches (Hirudinea) and snails (Mollusca: Gastropoda) were made from the littoral zone of each loch visited, by collecting all the specimens found on a sample of 100 stones. These stones were lifted randomly between the edge and 50 cm depth of water. The stones usually ranged in size from 10 cm to 20 cm in diameter. All specimens collected were placed in labelled tubes and brought back to the laboratory for identification. The information (Table 6) was subsequently assessed in relation to granite and 'control' sites (Rooke 1984).

Table 6. The occurrence of leeches (Hirudinea) and molluscs (Mollusca) at the lochs sampled during 1984. The numbers are counts per 100 littoral stones

Lochs	Hirudinea	Mollusca
Granite:		
% occurrence	32	16
minimum number	0	0
maximum number	21	24
mean	2.3	1.5
Control:		
% occurrence	83	50
minimum number	0	0
maximum number	6	12
mean	3.2	5.3

4.5 Loch fish

Each loch visited was gill netted if permission had been given, and full details of the methods used are given in Appendix 3. The fish caught were identified and measured for length and weight. They were subsequently sexed and samples of scales (for ageing) and flesh (for metal analysis) were taken. The stomach contents of a sub-sample of each catch were examined.

The aims of the gill netting were as follows.

i. To give information on the status of fish in the lochs and the size/age structure of the population, as acidification causes recruitment failures which distort both age structure and growth rates (Frenette & Dodson 1984).

ii. To provide stomach contents for analysis of the diet, because reduced fish predation (eg where acidification has lowered fish numbers) allows an increase in the numbers of invertebrate biota and their significance in fish diet increases correspondingly.

iii. To provide flesh samples for chemical analysis, because the long-range transportation of heavy metals or their local release through the acidification process may show up by their accumulation in fish tissues.

iv. To allow examination of fish for any pollution-induced deformities.

4.6 Stream fish

Establishing whether or not inflow and outflow streams are suitable for young salmonids, later to be recruited to the loch, was regarded as an important part of the study. The population structure of the nursery stream populations was also felt to be of considerable significance, as (at least for salmonids) it is these nursery streams which are most vulnerable to acid 'events' (Bjarnborg 1983), reflected years later by missing year classes in the loch.

At each loch, standard electro-fishing procedures, using portable battery-powered equipment, were carried out in both the major inflow and the outflow. Fishing was continued for a known period of time and the length and width of streams fished were noted. All fish caught were identified, measured for length and returned to the stream alive.

5 Principal results

The principal objective of this study was a relatively straightforward one: to what extent do fish populations in fresh waters in Scotland appear to have been affected by acid deposition? The approach adopted was to examine a large sample of a type of water known to be vulnerable to acidification—lochs with granite basins and catchments—and to study the status of fish in these lochs and their associated streams as well as in nearby 'control' systems, whose catchments were not on granite.

The detailed results of the project are considered in the individual scientific papers presented as Appendices to this report. Here, only the major conclusions relative to the initial objective are considered.

The main results are summarized in Table 7 and in Figure 2, where the values for pH and calcium are cross-plotted. Superimposed on these plots is the acidification curve proposed by Henriksen (1979) which assumes that, in acidified waters, bicarbonates are used up as acidity increases, leaving the calcium at a disproportionately higher level than normal. The curve indicates the normal relationship expected between the 2; any waters whose values are significantly above this curve are assumed to be acidified. In this way, 'acidified' waters can be distinguished from those which are naturally 'acid'.

According to the Scandinavian information, the more acidified a loch, the more likely it is to be fishless; it is evident from Figure 2 that most of the present data agree with this view. Of all the 52 granite sites examined, 14 (27%) were found to be fishless, whereas, of the 17 control lochs (excluding those on Islay), none were fishless. Similar results were obtained for fish populations in the inflow and outflow streams of these lochs. Though information is not available for all of them, it is known that the majority of these fishless lochs formerly had trout populations (Plate 2). The conclusion is that these lochs have become more acid in recent years and that this has caused the extinction of the fish.

There has been considerable controversy over the origin of the pollutants concerned and the actual nature of the acidification process (Brown & Sadler 1981; Howells 1983), but the present results certainly agree with the historical data presented by Flower and Battarbee (1983), Battarbee (1984) and others, for some of the sites which are now fishless.

How serious is the problem in Scotland? It is known from map counts that there are some 31460 lochs in Scotland as a whole but only 1536 (4.88%) have basins within granite. However, the majority (1159) are small lochs (less than 1 ha). This class was not examined. Only 279 lochs larger than one ha have basins and catchments lying entirely on granite; this number represents 0.89% of the Scottish total. These figures could be interpreted as indicating that, even if all these lochs are affected, acidification is not having a serious overall effect on fish and fresh waters.

The real situation is not so straightforward, however, for 2 principal reasons. First, there are notable differences in the way in which lochs on granite appear to be affected in different geographic areas (Figure 3). Thus, a very high proportion of the waters on granite in Galloway have become acidified and fishless over the last few decades, but practically none on granite in, say, the Criffel area (Plate 3), Rannoch Moor (Plates 4 & 5), Morvern (Plate 6) or Caithness (Plate 7). It must also be remembered that some waters may be

Table 7. Percentage of loch and stream sites at which the fish species recorded during this study were caught. The data refer only to the results from gill netting (lochs) and electro-fishing (streams)

Fish species	Lochs	Streams
Atlantic salmon (Salmo salar)	0	2
Brown trout (Salmo trutta)	68	65
Arctic charr (Salvelinus alpinus)	2	0
Pike (Esox lucius)	3	2
Minnow (Phoxinus phoxinus)	3	5
Roach (Rutilus rutilus)	2	0
Eel (Anguilla anguilla)	3	23
Three-spined stickleback (Gasterosteus aculeatus)	0	13
Nine-spined stickleback (Pungitius pungitius)	0	2
Perch (Perca fluviatilis)	3	0
Total number of species	7	7

fishless for reasons other than acidification (Plate 8). Second, although they may still contain fish, a number of waters appear to be partially acidified, and presumably the process is continuing. In many of these systems (eg Loch Grannoch, shown in Plates 9 & 10), the fish populations are already showing signs of disappearing and therefore an uncertain number of waters will be added to the fishless total, unless acidification is reversed by calcium applications or other measures of the kind already in progress at Loch Dee (Burns et al. 1984) and Loch Fleet (Central Electricity Generating Board 1985). Third, there are other types of base-poor rocks (eg schists); lochs with catchments on these are also vulnerable to acidification. Fourth, the extensive deposits of peat in many Scottish catchments and the consequent increase in the organic content of their waters must reduce the risk from aluminium toxicity, regardless of solid geology.

6 Conclusions

In summary, in only one part of Scotland—Galloway—do significant numbers of lochs appear to have been substantially affected by acidification. Here, 2 major blocks of granite (Doon and Cairnsmore) are involved. In total, there are 38 lochs on these blocks, 23 of which are more than one ha in area.

During this study, 11 of these 23 larger lochs were examined. It was concluded, from chemical data, that all of them were acidified (Henriksen 1979) and 6 were found to be fishless. Fish in the other 5 lochs showed signs of acid stress (tail deformities, fewer young fish, etc). It is assumed that the 12 lochs not examined are similarly affected by acidification, and, indeed, this

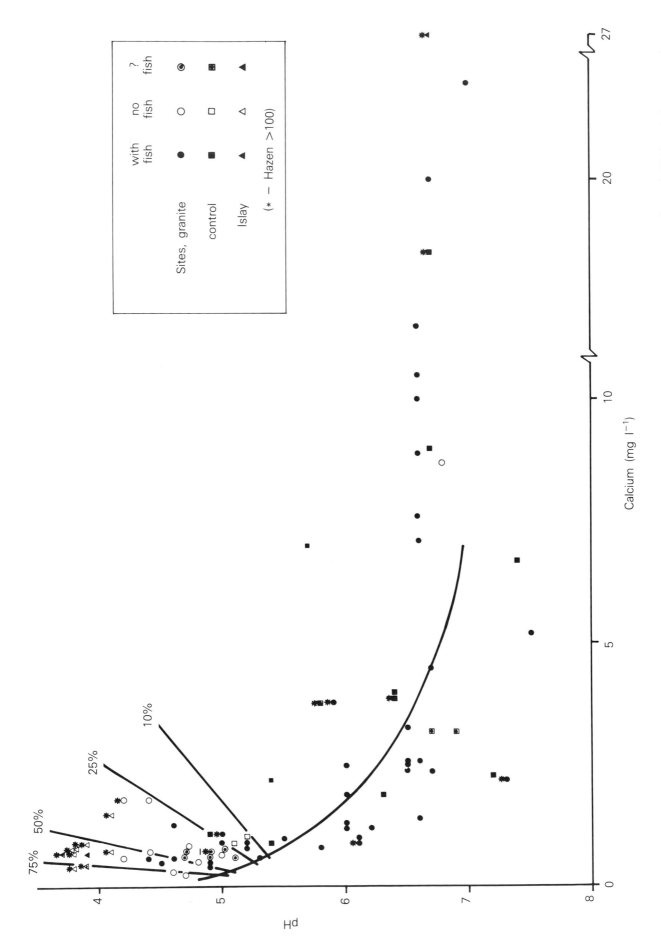

Figure 2. pH and calcium plots of lochs fished during this study, superimposed on the acidification curve of Henriksen (1979) and the proportions suggested likely to be fishless by Brown (1982), recalculated from Wright and Snekvic (1978). It should be noted that not all the sites shown are applicable to this curve because of their high organic content (*).

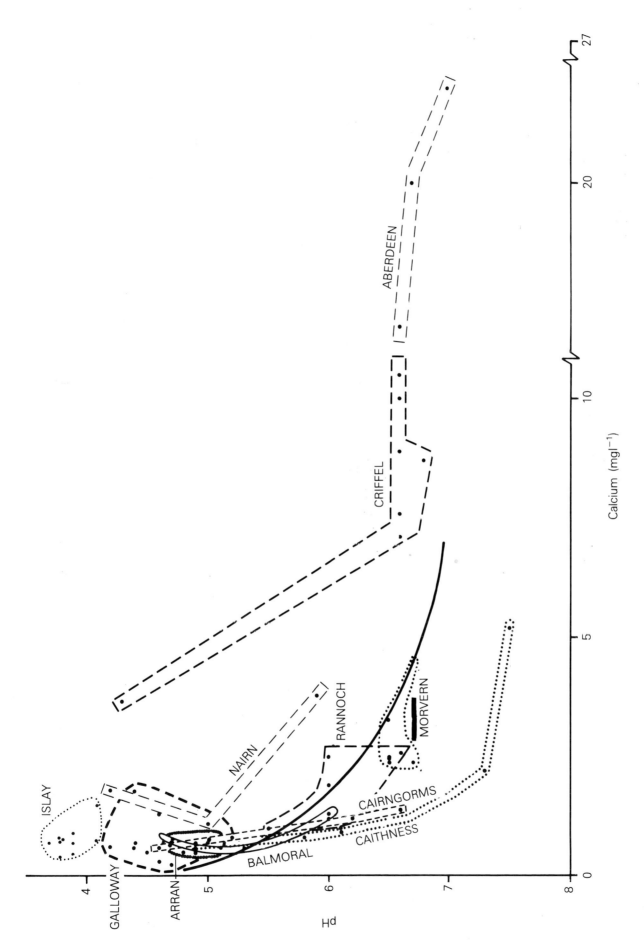

Figure 3. Geographic relationships of pH and calcium plots of all lochs on granite sampled during the project. Also shown is the Henriksen (1979) acidification curve, though it should be noted that not all the sites shown are applicable to this curve because of their high organic content.

appears to be the case from the data of other workers. Virtually all of them are acidified chemically (Wright & Henriksen 1980) and in several of them the fish populations are exhibiting acidification symptoms (Burns *et al.* 1984; Hay 1984).

Over the rest of Scotland there was very much less evidence of lochs on granite being significantly affected by acidification (Figure 4). In total, there are 354 lochs more than one ha in area on granites other than Doon and Cairnsmore. This study examined 38 of these lochs in 7 different areas—Morvern, Criffel, Rannoch, Caithness, Cairngorm, Balmoral and Aberdeen. The great majority of these appeared to show no signs of acidification, and only 4 were fishless. A similar situation appears to be likely for those lochs not examined.

The situation, however, is by no means a simple one. In addition to the lochs on granite, 11 'control' lochs were examined, and, although all of these lochs were found to contain fish, some of these (in Galloway at least) appeared to be acidified chemically. Thus, waters in areas of hard rock (slates and schists) other than granite are being affected, as has been found

with streams in the Loch Ard area (Harriman & Morrison 1981).

Extensive areas of peat in the catchment also modify the situation. Though these peats are in themselves fairly acid, they may control the effect of aluminium to a substantial extent so that fish are little affected. Some extremely acid, very stained, waters were found on Islay. Some were fishless but there was no evidence that they had ever had self-sustaining trout populations. One of the lochs, however, definitely did have fish in the past and has lost its population within the last century. Whether this loss was due to increased acidity from the surrounding peat or from atmospheric deposition is difficult to say in the present state of knowledge of the chemistry of humic waters as related to the acidification process (see also Appendix 5).

The main conclusion drawn from these results appears to be quite simple—some lochs on granite in Scotland have been acidified and become fishless over recent years, but these represent a small percentage of the Scottish total. The effect is localized and predominantly in south-west Scotland. In addition, some other

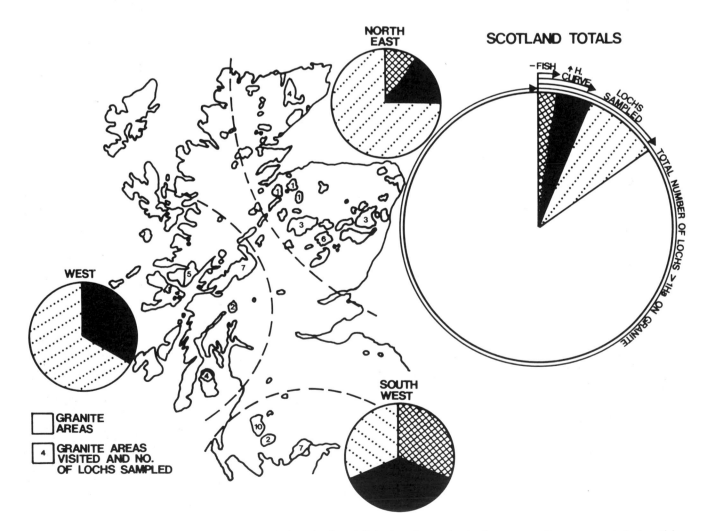

Figure 4. National and regional summary of chemical and fish data from the lochs on granite surveyed during this study. The figures within the blocks are the number of lochs surveyed there

Plate 1. Transporting sampling equipment to hill lochs in Galloway. Loch Enoch, lying at a height of 493 m, is 4 km away over the ridge on the horizon, and 3 other lochs there will be visited the same day (Photograph R N B Campbell)

Plate 2. Loch Valley in Galloway, previously a good loch for brown trout, is now fishless. The last 2 trout recorded from this loch were taken by the photographer in 1970. Beyond it can just be seen Loch Neldricken, which is also fishless now, but formerly held brown trout and pike (Photograph P S Maitland)

Plate 3. Duff's Loch in Galloway. Though lying entirely within the Criffel granite block, this loch, like most of the others in the block, appears to have sufficient buffering material in the catchment drift to counter acidification, for it supports a good population of brown trout and nine-spined sticklebacks (Photograph P S Maitland)

Plate 4. Dubh Loch ('Kingshouse N') on the Moor of Rannoch. One of the many peat-stained lochs on granite in this area, its waters, though brown and moderately acid, still manage to support a good population of brown trout (Photograph K H Morris)

Plate 5. Loch Mhic Pheadair Ruadh is one of the 'control' lochs in the study and lies entirely outside the neighbouring granites of the Moor of Rannoch. It supports a substantial population of brown trout and minnows (Photograph K H Morris)

Plate 6. Loch Tearnait in Morvern, Argyll. Though lying entirely on granite and with relatively clear water, it appears to be sufficiently buffered to maintain a good population of brown trout and three-spined sticklebacks (Photograph P S Maitland)

Plate 7. Loch Dubh Cul Na Beinne in Caithness is one of several brown-stained lochs on the granites in this area. Like most of them, it supports an excellent population of brown trout (Photograph P S Maitland)

Plate 8. Loch nan Eun on the Balmoral Estate in Grampian is a clear water loch lying entirely on granite and is apparently fishless. It is not known whether it has always been so or whether it at one time held brown trout (Photograph R N B Campbell)

Plate 9. Loch Grannoch in Galloway, which formerly supported an excellent fishery for brown trout and contained one of the few populations of arctic charr in south-west Scotland. The trout population has declined dramatically in the last 2 decades and the charr appear to have been extinct for some years (Photograph P S Maitland)

Plate 10. The outflow from Loch Grannoch in Galloway. Though this burn looks attractive with clear water, clean gravels and an exuberant growth of moss, it is no longer able to support any fish in its highly acid waters (Photograph P S Maitland)

Plate 11. Loch Enoch in Galloway was reported to have brown trout with deformed tails in 1882. The loch is now fishless—as are Loch nam Manaichean on Islay and Loch Fleet in Galloway, both of which once possessed trout with similar deformities (reported in 1872 and 1948 respectively) (Photograph P S Maitland)

Plate 12. The Round Loch of Glenhead in Galloway is one of several lochs in this area apparently still undergoing changes due to acidification. The brown trout population is sparse and many have deformed tails; only eels occur in the outflow burn (Photograph A A Lyle)

lochs are acidifying and are likely to lose their fish over the next one or 2 decades. Again, the number involved appears to be small.

A number of questions remains to be answered, however, and future research should be directed at these. What are the precise characteristics of the acidified (and acidifying) lochs (especially, say, in Galloway) which make them particularly vulnerable? What is the rate of acidification in those which are continuing to change, and what is the most appropriate way of monitoring this rate?

Other interesting areas of future research have also been revealed. What is producing the scattering effect on echo soundings from fishless lochs, and could a monitoring system be developed which is based on this phenomenon? Fish tail deformities may well be one of the earliest warnings that acidification is affecting fish; perhaps the value of this factor too could be assessed for future monitoring purposes. These topics are discussed further in Section 7.

7 Future research
During the relatively short 2-year study period of this project, it became apparent that certain chemical and biological features found in some of the sample lochs required further research, if their association with the acidification process was to be understood. Three of the most important of these features are discussed below.

During the echo sounding surveys for bathymetry, large numbers of echoes were recorded from the open water of those lochs which were thought to be acidified (from their chemistry) and fishless (from the netting). Due to a shortage of time and suitable equipment, it was not possible to identify the source of these echoes during the surveys. However, because of their high densities, their spatial distribution and some casual investigation, it is suggested that they are caused by invertebrates of some kind—possibly corixids, beetles or chironomid pupae.

A possible explanation is that, as fish decrease in number during the process of acidification and eventually disappear, their prey species often increase in number and spread into the formerly more vulnerable, open water, where the larger species can be detected by echo sounding. This feature was recorded in many of the acidified Galloway lochs, in Islay (where the lochs appear to be very acid from natural causes) and in some lochs in the Grampian Region.

A second interesting feature arising within the project came initially from the historic evidence of deformity in the tails of trout from acidified waters, possibly caused by acid episodes in spawning streams during embryological development. Past examples have been recorded from lochs in Galloway (1882, 1927 and 1940), one of these, for example, being Loch Enoch

(plate 11), and on Islay (1872). All the lochs concerned are now very acid and fishless; they are also among the highest in altitude in their area. In 1985, deformed trout were caught in acidified lochs in the same areas—for example, the Round Loch of Glenhead (Plate 12)—but at lower altitudes, suggesting a progression of acidification with decreasing altitude.

Both the Galloway and Islay lochs that produce or produced these similarly deformed trout are highly acid. They almost certainly differ, however, in the amount of the toxic inorganic aluminium which is present in their waters. Its level was probably high in the clear Galloway lochs but likely to be very low in the heavily organically stained Islay lochs. A common cause of these deformities would be the acidity itself—in Galloway from acid deposition but in Islay from either organic acids alone or combined with acid deposition—rather than anything associated with aluminium, or possibly other metal, toxicity. The physiological mechanism responsible is probably a distortion of the calcium metabolism, which has been associated with deformed non-salmonid fish in acidified lakes in North America. Studies of the features of this process and its incidence in various waters may establish them as valuable indicators of the start of the acidification of some systems.

Finally, an important area for future research is the whole question of the levels of aluminium and other elements in the chemical processes taking place, in clear acidified waters on the one hand and the many naturally acid, highly organically stained, waters on the other. A feature in which the fresh waters of Scotland seem to differ from those subject to acidification in both Scandinavia and North America is the high proportion of very organic waters in Scotland. This factor has important consequences for aluminium toxicity, because, of all the forms aluminium can take in solution, it is only the inorganic forms that are toxic to fish (Driscoll *et al.* 1980). However, the most toxic of these aluminium ions react strongly with organic molecules to form harmless organo-metallic compounds.

The level of toxicity of the other inorganic forms is unclear, as is their interaction, if any, with organic molecules, but Driscoll *et al.* (1980) have shown that, in waters with high dissolved organic content, organically bound aluminium is the predominant fraction of total aluminium. Because the formation of these organo-metallic complexes clears water of peat staining, presumably any water stained brown is free of the most toxic form of dissolved aluminium, and there are a great many such brown waters in the base-poor uplands of Scotland. The possibility is, therefore, that most of upland Scotland is protected, to some degree, from the effects of acidification by its peaty soils, whereas the mineral soils of parts of Scandinavia and North America offer no such protection to their waters. Thus, Scotland as a whole may be much less susceptible to loss of fish populations through acidification, even though the amount of acid deposited may be as great as elsewhere.

The lack of information about this process, particularly in relation to the valuable Henriksen (1979) acidification criteria for lochs, means that some of the lochs were not really suitable for the analyses described in this report. Further study of this aspect is required if peat-stained waters, of which there are many in Scotland, are not to be excluded from any overall appraisal of the impact of acidification. In addition, there are a number of important lochs which lie only partly on granite, but where this factor combines with others, in particular extensive afforestation, to lead to significant acidification. Loch Doon, which has the only remaining population of arctic charr in south-west Scotland, is such a loch, and as such merits further investigation.

8 References

Almer, B. 1974. Effects of acidification on Swedish lakes. *Ambio*, **3**, 30-36.

Anderson, J.G.C. 1939. *The granites of Scotland.* Edinburgh: HMSO.

Battarbee, R.W. 1984. Diatom analysis and the acidification of lakes. *Phil. Trans. R. Soc. B*, **305**, 193-219.

Beamish, R.J., Lockhart, W.L., Van Loon, J.C. & Harvey, H.H. 1975. Long term acidification of a lake and resulting effects on fishes. *Ambio*, **4**, 98-102.

Bjarnborg, B. 1983. Dilution and acidification effects during the spring flood of four Swedish mountain brooks. *Hydrobiologia*, **101**, 19-26.

Bobee, B. & Lachance, M. 1984. Multivariate analysis of parameters related to lake acidification in Quebec. *Wat. Resour. Bull.*, **20**, 545-556.

Brown, D.J.A. 1982. The effect of pH and calcium on fish and fisheries. *Water Air Soil Pollut.*, **18**, 343-351.

Brown, D.J.A. & Sadler, K. 1981. The chemistry and fishery status of acid lakes in Norway and their relationship to European sulphur emissions. *J. appl. Ecol.*, **18**, 433-431.

Burns, J.C., Coy, J.S., Tervet, D.J., Harriman, R., Morrison, B.R.S. & Quine, C.P. 1984. The Loch Dee Project: a study of the ecological effects of acid precipitation and forest management on an upland catchment in south-west Scotland. 1. Preliminary investigations. *Fish. Manage.*, **15**, 145-167.

Cape, J.N., Fowler, D., Kinnaird, J.W., Paterson, I.S., Leith, I.D. & Nicholson, I.A. 1984. Chemical composition of rainfall and wet deposition over northern Britain. *Atmos. Environ.*, **18**, 1921-1932.

Central Electricity Generating Board. 1985. *The Loch Fleet Project.* London: Central Electricity Generating Board.

Drablos, D. & Tollan, A. 1980. *Ecological impact of acid precipitation.* (SNSF Project 72/80.) Oslo: SNSF.

Driscoll, C.T., Baker, J.P., Bisogni, J.J. & Schofield, C.L. 1980. Effect of aluminium speciation on fish in dilute acidified waters. *Nature, Lond.*, **284**, 161-164.

Engblom, E. & Lingdell, P.E. 1983. Usefulness of the bottom fauna as a pH indicator. *SNV PM*, **1741**, 1-181.

Eriksson, M.O.G. 1984. Acidification of lakes: effects on waterbirds in Sweden. *Ambio*, **13**, 260-262.

Flower, R. & Battarbee, R.W. 1983. Diatom evidence for the recent acidification of two Scottish lochs. *Nature, Lond.*, **305**, 130-133.

Frenette, J.J. & Dodson, J.J. 1984. Brook trout (*Salvelinus fontinalis*) population structure in acidified Lac Tawtare. *Can. J. Fish. aquat. Sci.*, **41**, 865-877.

Haines, T.A. 1981. Acidic precipitation and its consequences for aquatic ecosystems: a review. *Trans. Am. Fish. Soc.*, **110**, 669-707.

Hakanson, L. 1981. *A manual of lake morphometry.* New York: Springer.

Harriman, R. & Morrison, B.R.S. 1980. Ecology of acid streams draining forested and non-forested catchments in Scotland. In: *Ecological impact of acid precipitation*, edited by D. Drablos & A. Tollan, 312-313. Oslo: SNSF.

Harriman, R. & Morrison, B.R.S. 1981. Forestry, fisheries and acid rain in Scotland. *Scott. For.*, **35**, 89-95.

Harriman, R. & Morrison, B.R.S. 1982. Ecology of streams draining forested and non-forested catchments in an area of central Scotland subject to acid precipitation. *Hydrobiologia*, **88**, 251-263.

Harriman, R. & Wells D.E. 1985. Causes and effects of surface water acidification in Scotland. *Wat. Pollut. Contr.*, **84**, 215-224

Harvey, H.H. 1975. Fish populations in a large group of acid stressed lakes. *Verh. int. verein. theor. angew. Limnol.*, **19**, 2406-2417.

Harvey, H.H. & Lee, C. 1982. Historical fisheries' changes related to surface water pH changes in Canada. In: *Acid rain/fisheries*, edited by R. E. Johnson, 45-54. New York: Cornell University.

Hay, D. 1984. Acid rain—the prospect for Scotland. *Proc. A. Study Course, Inst. Fish. Manage.*, **15**, 110-118.

Henriksen, A. 1979. A simple approach for identifying and measuring acidification of fresh water. *Nature, Lond.*, **278**, 542-545.

Henriksen, E. 1982. Susceptibility of surface waters to acidification. In: *Acid rain/fisheries*, edited by R. E. Johnson, 103-107. New York: Cornell University.

Henriksen, A., Skogheim, O.K. & Rosseland, B.O. 1984. Episodic changes in pH and aluminium-speciation kill fish in a Norwegian salmon river. *Vatten*, **40**, 255-260.

Howells, G.O. 1983. Fishery status and water quality in areas affected by acid deposition. *Water Sci. Technol.*, **15**, 67-80.

Johnson, R.E. 1982. *Acid rain/fisheries. Proc. int. Symp. on Acidic Rain and Fishery Impacts on Northeastern North America.* New York: Cornell University.

Macaulay Institute. 1982. *Soil survey of Scotland.* Aberdeen: Macaulay Institute for Soil Research.

McDonald, J. 1927. The tailless trout of Loch Enoch. *Trans. Proc. Dumfries. Galloway nat. Hist. Antiq. Soc.*, **67**, 299-308.

Mathews, R.O., McCaffrey, F. & Hart, E. 1984. Acid rain in Ireland. *Ir. J. environ. Sci.*, **1**, 47-50.

Muniz, I.P. & Leivestad, H. 1980. Acidification—effects on freshwater fish. In: *Ecological impact of acid precipitation*, edited by D. Drablos & A. Tollan, 84-92. Oslo: SNSF.

Murray, J. & Pullar, L. 1910. *Bathymetrical survey of the Scottish freshwater lochs.* Edinburgh: Challenger Office.

Overrein, L.N., Seip, H.M. & Tollan, A. 1980. *Acid precipitation—effects on forests and fish.* (SNSF Project 72/8.) Oslo: SNSF.

Peach, C.W. 1872. On the so-called tailless trout of Islay. *Rep. Br. Ass. Advmt Sci.*, **41**, 133-134.

Rooke, J.B. 1984. Mollusca of six low-alkalinity lakes in Ontario. *Can. J. Fish. aquat. Sci.*, **41,** 777-782.

Schofield, C.L. 1982. Historical fisheries changes in the United States related to decrease in surface water pH. In: *Acid rain/fisheries,* edited by R. E. Johnson, 57-61. New York: Cornell University.

Smith, I.R. & Lyle, A.A. 1979. *The distribution of fresh waters in Great Britain.* Cambridge: Institute of Terrestrial Ecology.

Stoner, J.H., Gee, A.S. & Wade, K.R. 1984. The effects of acidification on the ecology of streams in the upper Tywi catchment in west Wales. *Environ. Pollut. A,* **35,** 125-157.

Tome, M.A. & Pough, F.H. 1982. Responses of amphibians to acid precipitation. In: *Acid/rainfisheries,* edited by R. E. Johnson, 245-249. New York: Cornell University.

Traquair, R.H. 1882. On specimens of 'tailless' trout from Loch Enoch, in Kirkcudbrightshire. *Proc. R. phys. Soc. Edinb.,* **7,** 221-223.

United Kingdom Review Group on Acid Rain. 1983. *Acid deposition in the United Kingdom.* Stevenage: Warren Spring Laboratory.

United Kingdom Acid Waters Review Group. 1986. *Acidity in United Kingdom fresh waters.* London: Department of the Environment.

Watt Committee on Energy. 1984. *Acid rain.* London: Watt Committee on Energy.

Wright, R.F. & Henriksen, A. 1980. *Regional survey of lakes and streams in southwestern Scotland, April 1979.* (SNSF Project 72/80.) Oslo: SNSF.

Wright, R.F. & Snekvic, E. 1978. Acid precipitation—chemistry and fish populations in 700 lakes in southern-most Norway. *Verh. int. verein. theor. angew. Limnol.,* **20,** 765-775.

Wright, R.F., Conroy, N., Dickson, W., Harriman, R., Henriksen, A. & Schofield, C.L. 1980. Acidified lake districts of the world. In: *Ecological impact of acid precipitation,* edited by D. Drablos & A. Tollan, 377-379. Oslo: SNSF.

Appendix 1

The bathymetry and hydrology of some lochs vulnerable to acid deposition in Scotland

A A LYLE

Summary

Bathymetric surveys were carried out on previously unsurveyed Scottish lochs as part of a programme studying acidification. These surveys provided background information on the physical character of the sites and made possible a basic examination of relationships between water retention times and acidification. The results indicate that lochs with retention times of a few months are most likely to suffer from long-term acidification, but that longer-term chemical information is required for more definite conclusions.

1 Introduction

Information on the bathymetry of a loch is an important part of any study of its ecology. In the context of acidification research (Maitland *et al.* 1986), bathymetric information, together with catchment and climatic data, enables the calculation of theoretical retention time—an important hydrological parameter. Thereaf-ter, a differentiation between lochs can be made with regard to the impact and duration of influence of episodic acid inputs, in terms of hydrological para-meters, which may be used to identify their vulnerabil-ity to acidification.

A loch with a short average retention time of a few days may be completely flushed out during periods of heavy rainfall, particularly if this occurs after a pro-longed dry spell, when runoff is faster and loch levels (and therefore volumes) are low. Given the episodic nature of acid influxes, a rapid water replacement in such a loch could mean a dramatic change in the chemistry of the whole loch and the environment of its aquatic biota. Most likely, such an event would be short-lived, but, depending on its seasonal timing, considerable biological damage could be caused. Such a sequence of events would be unlikely in lochs which have retention times of, say, a few months, but an acidic input would obviously remain in such lochs for a

Plate 1. The boat and echo sounding equipment used during this study (Photograph P S Maitland)

longer time, perhaps leading to a slower but more stable period of acidification.

2 Methods

Echo sounding surveys were made from small boats (either fibreglass or inflatable) which were dragged or carried to the sites (plate 1). A compact, portable echo sounder and battery pack were fitted to a rucksack frame and also carried to the sites. The echo sounder used was a Lowrance X15A operating at 192 KHz with a 20° beam angle transducer, powered by a 12 volt dry cell battery. This equipment proved ideal for the bathymetry concerned because of its shallow depth capability and control flexibility, but on a few occasions, in very shallow waters of less than 0.5 m, measuring poles were needed.

At each site surveyed, echo sounding transects were run between identifiable points on the shore. Transect lines and end points were marked on to large-scale field maps. The number of transects taken varied according to loch size and morphometry, weather conditions and time constraints. At the smallest sites, only 4 or 5 transects were required, whereas the most

taken at any one site (Loch Valley) was 35—a total transect length of 6 km. The most demanding requirement of the surveys was to keep the transect lines straight and to row them at constant speed. This was difficult in a small boat in windy conditions. An assessment of the quality of each survey was made by calculating Hakanson's Information Value (I') (Hakanson 1981), although this Value does not take account of individual transect quality.

The time taken to survey individual lochs varied with their size. The smallest took about 30 minutes, whereas larger sites took up to one day. This figure does not include the time taken to carry equipment to the site, which was often several hours. The highest number of sites surveyed in a single 4-day field trip was 8 lochs (twice), but this was only possible where the sites were close together (eg Rannoch Moor) or there was easy access by road (eg Criffel).

Overall, new bathymetric information was obtained for 49 lochs, and existing data were available for 15 additional sites, mostly from Murray and Pullar (1910), making a total of 64 sites.

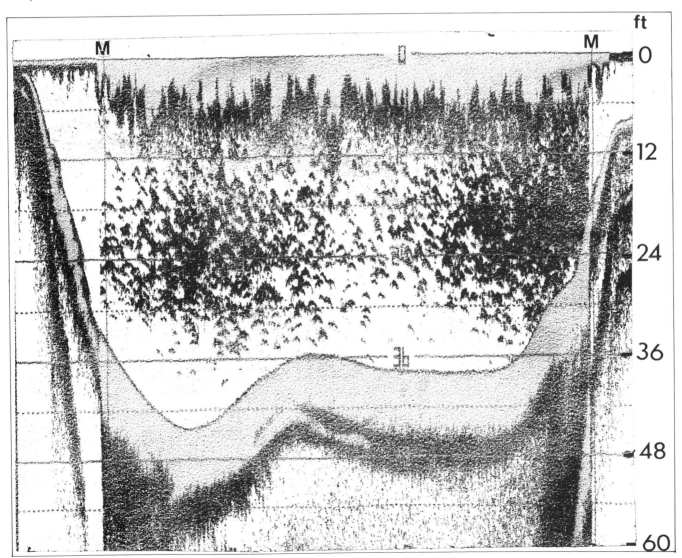

Plate 2. An echo trace from the fishless Loch Valley in Galloway, showing the unexpected dense echoes referred to in the text. M indicates changes in recording sensitivity

Base maps of all the lochs surveyed were produced by digitizing the loch shorelines and islands from 1:10000 scale OS maps. Once digitized, outline maps of the lochs could be made at suitable working scales. Echo sounding transects were marked on to these maps from the field reports. Depths were then plotted along the transects from the echo sounding charts (Plate 2), following the method described by Hakanson (1981), and illustrated in Figure 1. Finally, contour lines of equal depth were drawn on to the maps by eye (see Figure 1).

The areas within shorelines and depth contours were measured from maps by planimetry and, from them, loch volumes and mean depths were calculated. This calculation was done for the 49 lochs surveyed during the project, and equivalent information for the 15

remaining sites was obtained from the sources indicated in Table 1. Loch altitudes were estimated from the 1:10000 OS maps.

An approximation of the hydrological budget of the lochs was made by considering the loch volume, catchment area and net precipitation. This method is a simplification of any one situation, but by applying it to all the sites consistently it can identify broad similarities and differences in their hydrological regimes.

First, the topographical catchment area of each loch was defined from 1:25000 OS maps and measured by planimetry. In upland areas, the watershed is usually clear, but becomes progressively less so on flatter land forms, particularly peat bog areas such as Rannoch Moor.

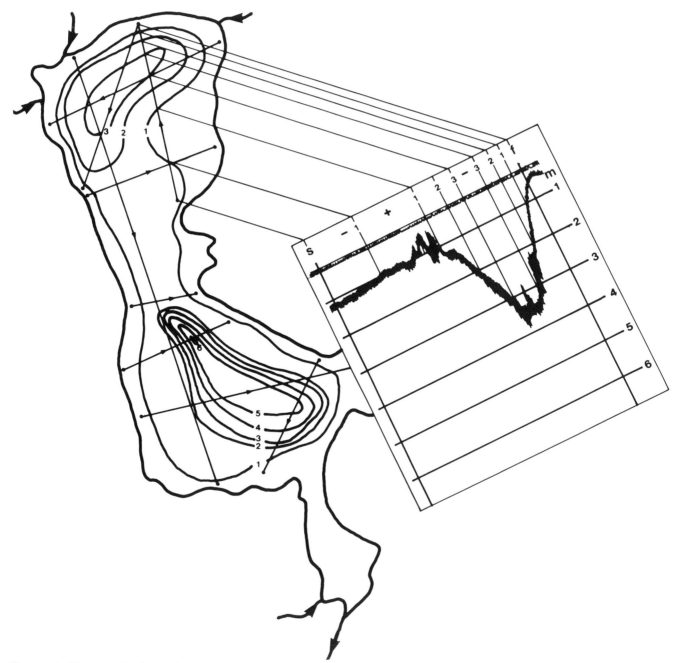

Figure 1. The method used to transfer depths along a transect line from the echo sounder charts to the bathymetric map (example: Long Loch of the Dungeon)

Table 1. Bathymetric data for the survey lochs

Number	Loch name	Data source	Altitude (m OD)	Loch area (ha)	Mean depth (m)	Survey I' value
1	Grannoch	M&P	211	117.30	6.35	—
2	Fleet	M&P	339	17.40	6.67	—
3	Lochenbreck	M&P	199	15.80	2.33	—
4	am Fhaing	BS	258	1.08	0.69	0.9960
5	nan Craobh	BS	238	3.61	0.72	0.9770
6	Tearnait	M&P	140	42.90	4.95	—
7	Dubha 'Morvern'	BS	204	6.03	0.85	0.9650
8	Caol	BS	249	2.46	0.96	0.9290
9	Uisge	BS	149	17.60	4.36	0.9277?
10	Mhic Pheadair Ruadh	est	303	1.13	0.40	—
11	Dubh 'Kingshouse W'	BS	302	3.32	0.32	—
12	Dubh 'Kingshouse N'	BS	311	3.20	0.90	—
13	Dubh 'Kingshouse E'	M&P	305	6.87	0.82	—
14	Mathair Eite	BS	296	15.80	0.72	0.9158
15	Gaineamhach	BS	294	27.20	1.42	0.9860?
16	Gaineamhach 'NE'	BS	296	11.20	0.60	0.9080
17	Gaineamhach 'SE'	est	292	1.70	0.15	—
18	Einich	JP	496	79.60	18.98	—
19	Beanaidh	BS	583	1.33	1.53	0.9510
20	Mhic Ghille-chaoil	BS	494	10.00	2.52	0.9940
21	Pityoulish	M&P	206	27.10	7.00	—
22	na Seilge	BS	119	56.00	1.79	0.9460
23	Talaheel	BS	187	6.80	0.71	0.9550?
24	nan Clach Geala	BS	193	7.70	1.14	0.9560
25	Dubh Cul Na Beinne	BS	189	6.38	0.67	0.9771
26	Tuim Ghlais	BS	165	40.30	1.21	0.9793
27	Long L of the Dungeon	BS	267	4.40	1.62	0.9400
28	Round L of the Dungeon	BS	275	4.50	3.68	0.9370
29	Enoch	ns	493	48.90	—	—
30	Arron	BS	445	2.70	1.03	0.9640
31	Neldricken	BS	348	32.90	4.29	0.8840
32	Dungeon	M&P	306	35.60	6.92	—
33	Narroch	BS	328	3.53	2.96	0.9484
34	Round L of Glenhead	B	295	12.50	4.29	—
35	Long L of Glenhead	BS	295	10.40	3.79	0.9652
36	Valley	BS	322	35.80	4.28	0.9249?
37	Harrow	M&P	247	15.40	3.49	—
38	Dow	ns	475	0.50	—	—
39	Dalbeattie Plantain	BS	27	3.07	2.72	0.9598
40	Fern	BS	83	5.89	1.43	0.9610
41	White	BS	33	12.00	4.10	0.9026
42	Barean	BS	44	9.42	3.65	0.9139
43	Clonyard	BS	42	4.71	3.11	0.9137
44	Fellcroft	BS	139	6.96	1.07	0.9627
45	Bengairn	BS	48	2.89	0.86	0.9672
46	Duff's	BS	41	1.23	1.47	0.9481
47	Kernsary	M&P	21	80.80	11.67	—
48	Ghiuragarstidh	M&P	36	23.40	2.78	—
49	Policies	BS	105	3.38	1.61	0.9596
50	Waterton	BS	101	1.93	1.06	0.9056
51	of Skene	M&P	84	119.00	1.43	—
52	Brandy	BBHS	637	27.30	22.44	—
53	Corby	BS	82	12.60	0.73	0.9546
54	Muick	M&P	400	222.20	35.31	—
55	Dubh 'Muick'	ns	638	19.30	—	—
56	Buidhe	BS	668	1.98	1.56	0.9600
57	Lochnagar	ns	785	10.36	—	—
58	nan Eun	BS	895	7.64	10.35	0.9246
59	Sandy	BS	792	4.71	1.04	0.9707
60	Bharradail	BS	99	3.97	1.45	0.9538
61	Beinn Uraraidh	BS	295	21.29	8.33	0.9478?
62	nam Breac	BS	362	5.16	4.16	0.9004
63	nam Manaichean	ns	—	—	—	—
64	Laoim	ns	—	—	—	—
65	Sholum	ns	—	—	—	—
66	Sholum 'W'	ns	—	—	—	—
67	Leorin 'W'	ns	—	—	—	—

68	Leorin 'E'	ns	—	—	—	—
69	na Beinne Brice	ns	—	—	—	—
70	'Moine na Surdaig'	ns	—	—	—	—
71	Coirre Fhionn	ns	—	—	—	—
72	Iorsa	ns	—	—	—	—
73	Garbad	ns	—	—	—	—
74	Cnoc an Loch	ns	—	—	—	—
75	a'Mhuillin	ns	—	—	—	—
76	Kirkaldy	BS	229	3.80	0.96	0.9685
77	a'Chaoruinn	BS	279	2.89	1.62	0.9323
78	an t'Sidhein	BS	355	8.10	1.79	0.9683
79	nan Stuirteag	BS	338	0.70	1.10	0.9722
80	a'Mhill Bhig	BS	475	3.46	0.75	0.9395
81	a'Mhill Bhig 'Lower'	BS	465	0.24	0.40	—
82	Maol Meadhonach 'Upper'	ns	490	0.40	—	—
83	Maol Meadhonach 'Lower'	ns	485	0.50	—	—

BS   = bathymetric survey
M&P = Murray and Pullar (1910)
JP   = J Pytches (pers. comm.)
BBHS = Bell Baxter High School (pers. comm.)
B   = R Battarbee (pers. comm.)
est = estimate from site visit
?   = doubtful survey
ns   = no survey

Average annual rainfall over the catchments was taken from the Meteorological Office map for the period 1941–70. Water losses to the atmosphere were estimated from tables of potential transpiration (Ministry of Agriculture, Fisheries & Food 1967) which incorporate an altitude correction. A standard approximate mean catchment altitude was used for this correction and was taken to be one third of the catchment range above loch level. Evaporation from loch surfaces was taken as 1.2 times the tabulated potential transpiration (see Penman 1948). The approximate net runoff volume is therefore the product of net precipitation and catchment (including loch) area.

Theoretical retention time (RT) is the end product of this approach and is calculated by:

365/(RUNOFF VOLUME/LOCH VOLUME)

and expressed as a number of days.

3 Results
The primary information is presented in Table 1, which gives the morphometric data for each site resulting from the bathymetric surveys and from other sources, which are identified. This information is not available for all 83 sites as surveys were prevented or curtailed on some by bad weather, and others were sampled only for water chemistry.

There is a considerable range in the size and type of loch included in the survey (Plate 3), from peat pools to large valley lochs, from shallow silty depressions to very steep-sided basins, and from lowland recreational sites to isolated alpine lochans. Some are totally artificial or have some throughflow control, but the majority are entirely natural. The extreme ranges from

Table 1 are:

Areas (ha)	0.24	222.20
Maximum depths (m)	0.60	78.00
Mean depths (m)	0.15	35.31
Volumes (m^3 × 10^3)	1.00	78,466.4
Altitudes (m OD)	21	895

An assessment of the quality of the bathymetric surveys conducted during this study was made by calculating part of the Hakanson Information Value (I' in Table 1) (Hakanson 1981):

$$I' = \frac{1}{A} \left[A - \left(0.14 \times \frac{A}{L} \times F^2 \times \sqrt{\frac{1}{n+a}} \times \sum_{i=1}^{n} \sqrt{a_{i-n}} \right) \right]$$

where: A = loch area, L = transect length, F = shoreline development, n = number of contours, and a = contour area.

In general, the I' values obtained were high and indicate that the amount of work carried out on the sites should produce satisfactory representations of bathymetry. However, this calculation, as it must do, neglects the quality of echo sounding transects in terms of uniform velocity and straightness. As mentioned earlier, wind—which affects both these requirements—was the major difficulty encountered on the surveys, and so only a subjective assessment of the real quality of each survey can be made by the surveyor. No systematic attempt has been made at such an assessment, but lochs where there is some doubt have been identified in Table 1.

Water retention time (RT) and the parameters required for its calculation are given in Table 2. Again, all the necessary information is not available for all the survey lochs, but a calculation has been made for 64 lochs.

Plate 3. Among the most difficult sites to survey were shallow rocky waters, such as Loch Gaineamhach on the Moor of Rannoch (Photograph K H Morris)

i.   ii.

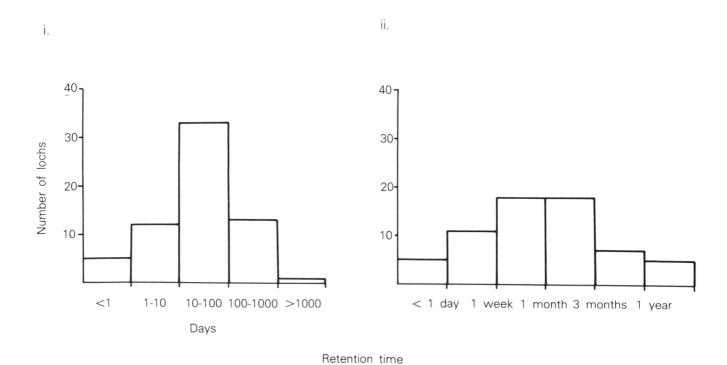

Figure 2. The frequency distribution of retention time for 64 of the survey lochs: (i) in logarithmic groups of days, and (ii) on a calendar scale to illustrate more ecologically relevant periods

There is a considerable range in mean RT for these lochs from 1.2 hours (Plate 4) to 4.25 years (Plate 5). Figure 2 shows the distribution of RT. Figure 2i is plotted against a logarithmic RT scale and shows the predominant category to be between 10 and 100 days, which accounts for 52% of the sites.

In Figure 2ii, RT is plotted against a calendar scale to illustrate more ecologically relevant water quality stability periods. For example, lochs in the longest category have an RT greater than one year, so slow long-term changes in their water quality associated with annual or longer variations in inflow quality would be expected. Those between 3 months and one year should have stability beyond seasonal trends, but most lochs fall into the next 2 lower categories and will follow monthly or weekly variations. The 2 lowest categories, less than one week, and less than one day, are those most susceptible to large and relatively rapid fluctuations in water quality and, indeed, to large proportional changes in their actual water retention times (see discussion below).

Chemical results from the inflow and outflow streams (2 sets taken, usually on consecutive days) were used to examine retention time effects on changes between inflow and outflow acidity. Figure 3 shows the relative differences for each sample set plotted against RT. Hypothetically, sampling over suitable periods would show such differences increasing with RT, but to some extent basing such calculations on spot samples introduces an element of chance. Also, the influence of other inflow streams is not taken into account. For example, at Loch Grannoch (RT = 98.2 days), pH was measured on 3 separate visits (May and December 1984, and May 1985). Outflow pH was fairly constant (4.6, 4.3 and 4.6 respectively), but inflow pH was not (6.2, 4.5 and 4.8) and hence the differences (1.6, 0.2 and 0.2) could vary markedly. So, although the distribution of points in Figure 3 partly supports the hypothesis, longer chemical records are required for a reliably informative relationship.

If consideration of RT is confined to those lochs assumed to be fully vulnerable to acidification (ie excluding peaty and alkaline lochs—see Table 2 and Appendix 3), then there is a highly statistically significant difference between the RT of lochs above and below the Henriksen (1979) curve (see Section 4) at the 1% level (P=0.01). The respective means for RT for those groups are 143.0 days (n=22) and 62.2 days (n=19), although the standard deviations are large, being 319.0 and 147.0 respectively. Median values are 74.8 and 9.7 days.

Another, though related, concept is to examine the ratios of catchment area/loch area of the above-mentioned group of lochs on the basis that this

Plate 4. Loch Gaineamhach ('SE') on the Moor of Rannoch. This small and shallow loch has the shortest theoretical retention time (1.2 hours) of any of the survey lochs (Photograph K H Morris)

Plate 5. Loch Brandy in Angus, one of the 'control' sites in the study. This deep corrie loch has the longest theoretical retention time (4.25 years) of any of the survey lochs (Photograph K H Morris)

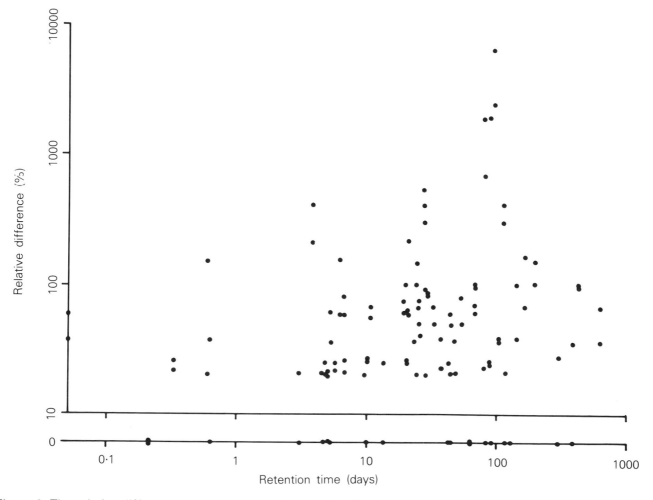

Figure 3. The relative difference in inflow and outflow acidity (ie the inflow, outflow difference in H^+ μeq l^{-1} as a percentage of the inflow value) for each chemistry sample set plotted against retention time

Table 2. Hydrological data for the survey lochs

Number	Loch name	Loch volume (m^{3}10^{-3})	Catchment area (ha)	Annual rainfall (mm)	Potential evaporation (mm)	Total runoff (m^{3}10^{-3})	Retention time (days)	'Acidifiable' lochs
1	Grannoch	7447.6	1334.00	2300	386	27687	98.20	A
2	Fleet	1161.0	107.60	2100	386	2129	199.00	A
3	Lochenbreck	368.1	129.20	1600	434	1677	80.10	A
4	am Fhaing	7.5	25.82	2300	518	478	5.70	B
5	nan Craobh	25.9	102.69	2400	518	1997	4.70	B
6	Tearnait	2123.8	1016.50	2200	518	17775	43.60	B
7	Dubha 'Morvern'	51.1	118.97	2000	518	1846	10.10	B
8	Caol	23.7	45.04	2400	518	891	9.70	B
9	Uisge	766.9	874.90	2900	518	21241	13.20	B
10	Mhic Pheadair Ruadh	4.5	239.47	2500	338	5201	0.32	B
11	Dubh 'Kingshouse W'	10.7	293.58	2550	312	6643	0.59	B
12	Dubh 'Kingshouse N'	28.8	16.80	2200	389	360	29.20	A
13	Dubh 'Kingshouse E'	56.6	27.53	2200	389	618	33.40	B
14	Mathair Eite	114.0	411.70	2300	373	8226	5.10	B
15	Gaineamhach	386.7	304.10	2100	366	5725	24.70	B
16	Gaineamhach 'NE'	67.2	457.60	2100	357	8163	3.00	B
17	Gaineamhach 'SE'	2.6	1082.20	2200	369	19845	0.05	B
18	Einich	15107.0	1106.7	1800	229	18600	296.40	B
19	Beanaidh	20.4	41.17	1500	255	528	14.10	B
20	Mhic Ghille-chaoil	252.4	74.40	1500	293	1013	91.00	A
21	Pityoulish	1897.2	667.90	900	367	3684	187.90	—
22	na Seilge	1003.2	324.60	1000	405	2219	165.00	—
23	Talaheel	48.2	35.70	1000	390	254	69.30	B
24	nan Clach Geala	87.7	51.70	1000	387	358	89.40	A
25	Dubh Cul Na Beinne	42.8	78.62	1000	381	521	30.00	—
26	Tuim Ghlais	485.9	1084.70	1000	389	6842	25.90	—
27	Long L of the Dungeon	71.2	215.00	2150	400	3836	6.80	A
28	Round L of the Dungeon	165.4	64.90	2010	402	1112	54.30	A
29	Enoc	—	160.50	2350	348	4158	—	A
30	Arron	27.8	22.30	2350	374	492	20.60	A
31	Neldricken	1410.8	423.40	2200	385	8257	62.40	A
32	Dungeon	2463.6	621.00	2350	376	12935	69.50	A
33	Narroch	104.6	74.57	2200	404	1400	23.30	A
34	Round L of Glenhead	536.3	85.60	2200	407	1749	111.90	A
35	Long L of Glenhead	393.9	89.00	2200	414	1767	81.40	A
36	Valley	1533.8	668.00	2200	404	12611	44.40	A
37	Harrow	538.0	367.70	2250	388	7121	27.60	A
38	Dow	—	3.90	2200	367	80	—	A
39	Dalbeattie Plantain	83.4	182.53	1200	532	1237	24.60	A
40	Fern	84.1	186.61	1350	532	1568	19.60	—
41	White	492.5	180.50	1200	532	1273	141.20	—
42	Barean	343.7	40.58	1200	532	324	387.20	—
43	Clonyard	146.5	75.29	1200	532	529	101.00	—
44	Fellcroft	74.6	104.94	1400	532	964	28.20	—
45	Bengairn	24.8	154.01	1400	532	1359	6.70	—
46	Duff's	18.1	186.27	1200	532	1251	5.30	—
47	Kernsary	9429.6	2136.20	1700	485	26858	128.10	—
48	Ghiuragarstidh	651.3	203.20	1700	485	2730	87.10	B
49	Policies	54.3	86.02	900	418	428	46.30	—
50	Waterton	20.5	2428.77	900	394	12298	0.61	—
51	of Skene	1699.0	3259.10	900	414	16319	38.00	—
52	Brandy	6126.0	100.20	1400	258	1442	1550.60	A
53	Corby	91.9	305.50	900	499	1263	26.60	—
54	Muick	78466.4	3521.60	1500	263	46194	620.00	B
55	Dubh 'Muick'		841.30	1600	221	11859	—	A
56	Buidhe	30.9	176.12	1600	220	2457	4.60	B
57	Lochnagar	—	93.44	1600	186	1464	—	A
58	nan Eun	790.9	39.26	1600	175	666	433.70	A
59	Sandy	48.9	258.39	1600	215	3642	4.90	B
60	Bharradail	57.7	211.03	1450	542	1948	10.80	—
61	Beinn Uraraidh	1772.4	91.21	1400	542	942	686.60	—
62	nam Breac	214.7	58.84	1600	542	672	116.70	A
63	nam Manaichean	—	1.70	1600	542	25	—	—
64	Laoim	—	—	—	—	—	—	—
65	Sholum	—	—	—	—	—	—	—
66	Sholum 'W'	—	—	—	—	—	—	—
67	Leorin 'W'	—	—	—	—	—	—	—

68	Leorin 'E'	—	—	—	—	—	—	—
69	na Beinne Brice	—	—	—	—	—	—	—
70	'Moine na Surdaig'	—	—	—	—	—	—	—
71	Coirre Fhionn	—	—	—	—	—	—	A
72	Iorsa	—	—	—	—	—	—	A
73	Garbad	—	—	—	—	—	—	—
74	Cnoc an Loch	—	—	—	—	—	—	—
75	a'Mhuillin	—	—	—	—	—	—	A
76	Kirkaldy	36.3	126.80	880	415	604	21.90	—
77	a'Chaoruinn	46.7	853.41	870	355	4408	3.90	—
78	an t'Sidhein	144.6	190.00	900	351	1082	48.80	—
79	nan Stuirteag	7.7	24.90	900	362	137	20.50	—
80	a'Mhill Bhig	25.8	52.14	3000	325	1485	6.30	A
81	a'Mhill Bhig 'Lower'	1.0	63.46	3000	308	1715	0.21	A
82	Maol Meadhonach 'Upper'	—	2.10	2700	—	67	—	A
83	Maol Meadhonach 'Lower'	—	48.30	2700	—	1318	—	A

A = above Henriksen curve
B = below Henriksen curve
— = excluded

evaluates them according to the proportional amounts of rain passing through the catchments to that falling directly on to the loch. Again, the differences between the groups are highly significant at the 1% level (P=0.01), the mean ratios being 26:1 (n=23) for lochs above the curve and 73:1 (n=19) for those below the curve. The respective median values are 9:1 and 26:1. The relevance of these relationships is discussed below.

4 Discussion
The results of the bathymetric surveys have made possible a brief examination of the possible influence of basic hydrological factors on the acidification status of the sample lochs. While the water chemistry sampling programme was not ideal for such analyses, there is some evidence of a relationship within the vulnerable oligotrophic group of lochs, separated by the Henriksen (1979) criteria for acidified waters. Two comparisons were found to be highly significant.

The simpler concept is the comparison of the proportional amounts of catchment-affected and direct rainfall entering a loch. (Low groundwater input has

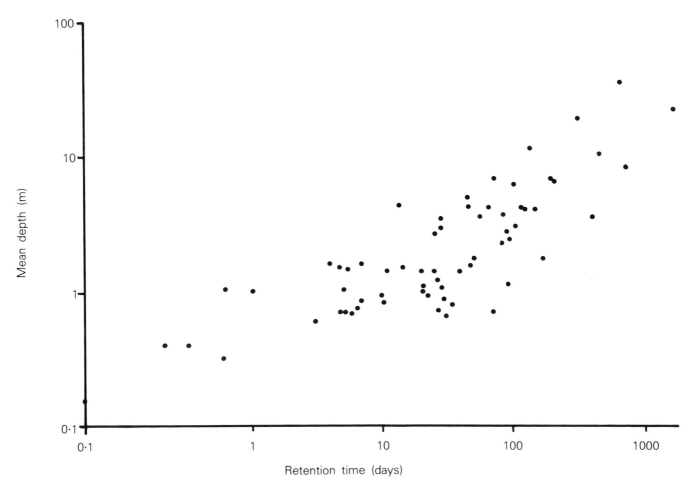

Figure 4. A plot of mean depth against retention time for the survey lochs

32

been shown to be a common feature of susceptible lakes in North America (Eilers 1983).) Although none of the sites approaches parity on this score, and they are all, to varying degrees, dominated by through-catchment water, the closest ratio of 3.28:1 belongs to Loch Enoch, an acidified fishless loch. In the short term, if the loch volume/area ratio (ie mean depth) is low, and catchment runoff response is slow, then there could be a direct rainfall-induced acidic 'pulse' in the loch, but such sites would normally be expected to have a short RT and catchment-affected water would soon dominate. Figure 4 illustrates the trend of decreasing RT with lower mean depths. However, it is also clear that shallow (say <1 m) lochs have RTs of up to 100 days, thus lengthening the period of direct rainfall influence.

Second, if the catchment runoff becomes acidified, however, then the stronger influence will be exercised by loch throughflow characteristics, considered here by retention time. As RT decreases, the greater is the similarity between a loch and its current inflow water quality and variability. With longer RT, loch water quality gains a stability beyond inflow fluctuations and becomes increasingly affected by changes which take place within the loch itself, related to normal seasonal and annual trends in its physical and biological characteristics.

Although the above deals with 2 different hydrological concepts, RT and loch catchment area/loch area ratio are themselves strongly interrelated (see Figure 5) and their relationships with the acidity of the survey lochs are perhaps inseparable without more detailed study.

The biological importance of RT can be expressed similarly to that for water quality. Lochs with a short RT and whose hydrodynamics are dominated by their inflows provide little escape or dilution for biota from acidic influxes, but these last for only a short time. A longer RT should make avoidance easier within the loch where fish may select 'favoured' areas away from the direct influence of inflows (see Muniz & Leivestad 1980). Also, there will probably be a considerable dilution of inputs. However, if the frequency of inflow acidifications is such that the effects within the loch overlap temporally, then acidity will accumulate in the loch, and this acidity may reach dangerous levels for long periods. A summary of this relationship is illustrated in Figure 6. It is assumed here that the lochs are subjected to acidic inputs, but the frequency and intensity of these inputs are not known. However, it seems reasonable to assume that, if RT is greater than (say) one year, then dilution of isolated acidic runoff will negate its toxicity. So, lochs most vulnerable to prolonged acidification and chemical and biological change are those with an RT of one to a few months.

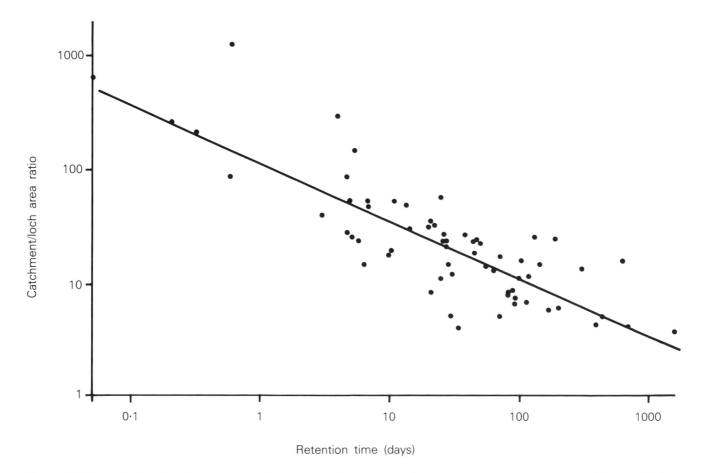

Figure 5. The relationship between catchment area/loch area ratio and retention time, where C/L = 118.4 × RT$^{-0.51}$ and the correlation coefficient is −0.83

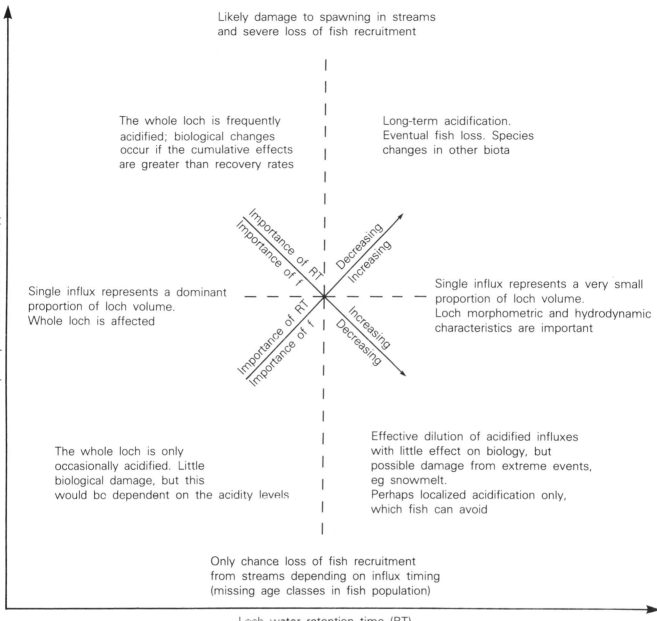

Figure 6. A diagrammatic summary of the relationship between loch retention time, the frequency of acidic inputs and the biological effects in lochs vulnerable to acidification

This range covers the majority of lochs involved in the survey and includes the Galloway lochs which, as a group, are considered to be those most severely acidified and, consequently, to have lost their fish.

This analysis has relied on generalities, and it is important to note that retention time should be regarded as a variable. The calculations used here are estimates of the mean, over a number of years. The longer the estimated RT, the more realistic is it likely to be at a given time. Lochs with a short RT may fluctuate greatly from their mean; indeed, a rough guide for natural drainage systems is that the average flow is only equalled or exceeded for *ca* 30% of the time. Many other factors will influence RT at any given time: catchment runoff characteristics; inflow/outflow locations; exposure to wind-driven mixing; summer thermal stratifications; ice cover and sudden flooding (eg snowmelt).

While it cannot be shown within the scope of this survey that morphometry or hydrology is a strongly limiting factor for acidification, consideration of this aspect has indicated that they must contribute to the already very complex set of circumstances which determine the extent to which the chemistry and biology of a loch are affected.

5 References

Drablos, D. & Tollan, A. 1980. *Ecological impact of acid precipitation.* (SNSF Project 72/80.) Oslo: SNSF.

Eilers, J. 1983. Hydrologic control of lakes' susceptibility to acidification. *Can. J. Fish. aquat. Sci.,* **40,** 1896-1904.

Hakanson, L. 1981. *A manual of lake morphometry.* New York: Springer.

Henriksen, A. 1979. A simple approach for identifying and measuring acidification of freshwater. *Nature, Lond.,* **278,** 542-545.

Maitland, P. S., Lyle, A. A. & Campbell, R. N. B. 1986. *The status of fish populations in waters likely to have been affected by acid deposition in Scotland.* Natural Environment Research Council contract report to the Department of Environment and the Commission of the European Communities. Edinburgh: Institute of Terrestrial Ecology. (Unpublished.)

Ministry of Agriculture, Fisheries & Food. 1967. *Potential transpiration.* (Technical bulletin no. 16.) Edinburgh: Department of Agriculture and Fisheries for Scotland.

Muniz, I. & Leivestad, H. 1980. Acidification—effects on freshwater fish. In: *Ecological impact of acid precipitation,* edited by D. Drablos & A. Tollan, 84-92. Oslo: SNSF.

Murray, J. & Pullar, L. 1910. *Bathymetrical survey of the Scottish freshwater lochs.* Edinburgh: Challenger Office.

Penman, H. 1948. Natural evaporation from open water, bare soil and grass. *Proc. R. Soc.,* **193,** 120-145.

Appendix 2

The chemical status of some lochs vulnerable to acid deposition in Scotland

P S MAITLAND, A A LYLE and R N B CAMPBELL

Summary
Water samples for chemical analysis were taken from the inflow and outflow streams of 83 Scottish lochs. Fifty-seven of these lochs had granite basins and catchments, whereas the catchments of the other 26 'control' lochs were of other types of bedrock. Samples were taken on 2 different occasions at each site. They were analysed for colour, pH, conductivity, calcium, magnesium, phosphorus, nitrogen, chloride and sulphur. The levels of these determinands found at each site are presented and discussed. Samples taken at different times from the same stream were always very similar and usually those from the inflow and outflow of each loch were too, although there were one or 2 notable exceptions. There was a general similarity among samples from the same geographic area but wide differences between some geographic areas. pH and calcium data, in relation to the curve proposed by Henriksen (1979), indicated that a number of sites could be regarded as acidified. The majority of these sites are in Galloway.

1 Introduction

Although considerable attention has been given to the chemistry of fresh waters in various parts of the world in relation to acidification (Vangenechten 1980; Wright *et al.* 1980; Brown & Sadler 1981; Bobee & Lachance 1984), relatively little information is yet available for Scotland, where the levels of acid deposition are known to be just as high as those in Scandinavia and North America (Cape *et al.* 1984). Though the main emphasis of the study of which this is part has been on the biology of the fish, a considerable number of chemical samples was taken during the survey and the results from their analyses are presented and discussed here.

Most attention within the project has been given to lochs whose basins and catchments lie on granite bedrock—much of the present evidence suggests that these sites are likely to be among the most vulnerable to acid deposition (Almer 1974), and that some of them at least have been acidifying since the Industrial Revolution (Flower & Battarbee 1983; Battarbee 1984). However, a number of 'control' lochs (whose basins and catchments lie on non-granitic rocks) were included in the study series also, for comparison.

2 Methods

Eighty-three lochs in the study series selected from maps were visited during 1984 and 1985. At each loch, water samples were taken from the major inflowing stream and the outflow, at the beginning and again at the end of each trip (Plate 1). The time interval involved here was usually one day, but occasionally 2 or 3 days. Water from the outflow was assumed to be representative of the loch itself.

Samples were always taken in the same way, using 250 ml bottles. Each bottle was rinsed twice using site water and then filled from just below the surface, making sure that no contaminant materials from the surface or elsewhere entered the bottle. Each sample was then kept dark and as cool as possible (but not frozen) until analysis.

Analysis of the determinands shown in Table 1 was carried out on each sample. For various reasons it was not possible to sample streams at all 83 loch sites. Several lochs had no evident inflows, a few had no running outflow at the time of the visit, or both were completely silted or dried up. Groundwater was assumed to be especially important to such systems (Anderson & Bowser 1986). Where inflow or outflow could not be sampled for any reason, 'substitute' samples were taken in the loch close to the most likely inflow and outflow during wet weather.

3 Chemistry

The general nature of the results of the chemical analyses are indicated in Figure 1 for all the determinands, with the exception of phosphorus and nitrogen. The values for both of these were extremely low at the great majority of sites and they are not discussed further here. A general point to note is that for several determinands there appears to be little difference between the distribution of the data from the granite lochs and those from the 'control' lochs. In general,

Table 1. Chemical determinands measured in this study

1.	Hazen colour
2.	pH
3.	Conductivity
4.	Calcium
5.	Magnesium
6.	Aluminium
7.	PO_4 phosphorus
8.	NO_3 nitrogen
9.	NH_4 nitrogen
10.	Chloride
11.	SO_4 sulphur

Plate 1. Taking a sample of the water in one of the burns visited during the study for subsequent chemical analyses (Photograph R N B Campbell)

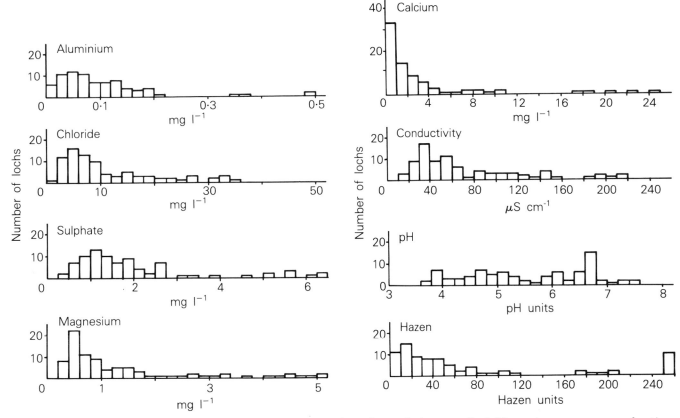

Figure 1. The frequency distribution of chemical determinands at all sites studied. The values are means for the outflow from each loch

too, there are few major differences between values from the inflow and outflow samples taken at any one loch (Figures 2 & 3).

The pH of most of the waters lay between 4.0 and 7.0, though a number of samples were below 4.0 (mainly the organically stained lochs on Islay) and a few above 7.0. Calcium levels were mostly low (the great majority less than 5.0 mg l^{-1}) with only 5 sites greater than 15 mg l^{-1}, and values for magnesium were all less than 5 mg l^{-1} with the exception of 2 sites.

As might be expected, the distribution of the values of chloride was similar to that of total conductivity, the majority of sites falling between 2.0–10.0 mg l^{-1} and 10-70 μS cm^{-1} respectively. Sites with the highest values were fairly obviously those nearest the sea and likely to be affected by windblown salts.

Values for Hazen were mostly less than 100 units, indicating rather clear water for the most part, but a few sites were exceptional in being over 250 units. These stained lochs were on Arran, Islay and Nairn.

Levels of total aluminium were almost all less than 0.2 mg l^{-1} but 5 lochs were, exceptionally, above this figure. Similarly, levels of sulphate were mostly low (the majority less than 5 mg l^{-1}) but there were a few sites with moderately high values. Sulphate is reduced in organically stained acid waters so the values from such waters (eg those on Islay) are not realistic.

One of the most interesting aspects of the chemistry in connection with the acidification problem lies in the values of pH and calcium in relation to the 'acidification curve' proposed by Henriksen (1979). Data from the present study are shown in Figure 4, and it is clear that there are a number of sites (mostly with pH values of less than 5.0) which would be classified as being acidified according to this criterion, although on a purely chemical basis it is important to look at other determinands as well (Brown 1982).

In looking more closely at the distribution of the sites in Figure 5, it can be seen that, in many cases, there is a close similarity between the chemistry of sites from the same geographic area, and that there are widely differing values from different areas. Thus, the lochs on Islay and in Galloway have low pH and calcium levels (Plate 2), whereas those from Criffel, Nairn (Plate 3) and Aberdeen have very much higher values for these determinands and would not be classified as acidified. However, only the Galloway lochs would be considered by Henriksen (1979) to be acidified, for he points out that his hypothesis is relevant to clear waters only and not to organically stained systems such as those on Islay.

4 Discussion
In view of the potential importance of episodic events (Bjarnborg 1983), the low numbers of water samples which it was possible to take during this study (one pair at the inflow and at the outflow of each loch) mean

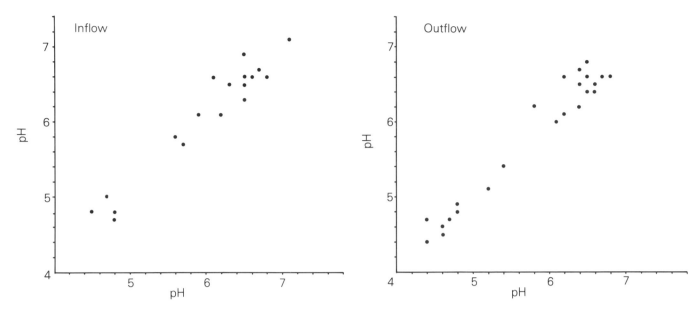

Figure 2. The distribution of cross-plots of pH values from pairs of samples taken from the inflows and the outflows of the lochs studied during 1984

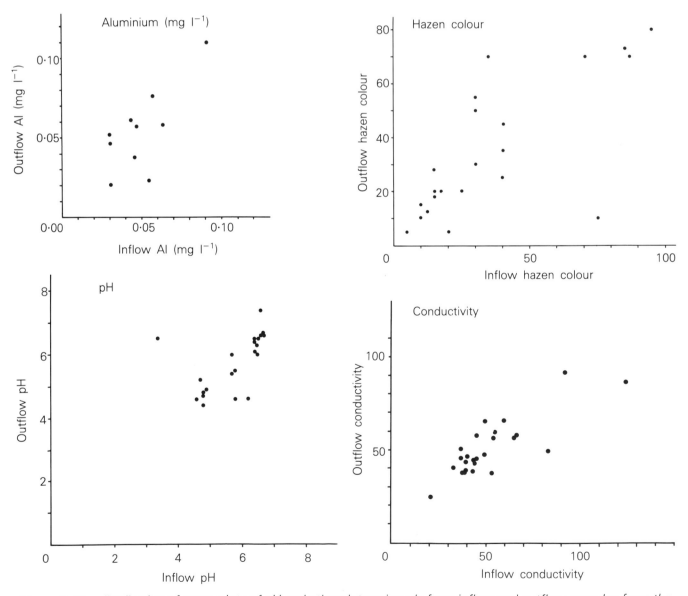

Figure 3. The distribution of cross-plots of pH and other determinands from inflow and outflow samples from the sites studied during 1984

Plate 2. The Long Loch of the Dungeon in Galloway, one of several lochs in this area which, though now partially acidified, still maintains a population of brown trout (Photograph R N B Campbell)

Plate 3. Loch Kirkaldy near Nairn, where there is no evidence yet of chemical acidification and the brown trout population is large and healthy (Photograph R N B Campbell)

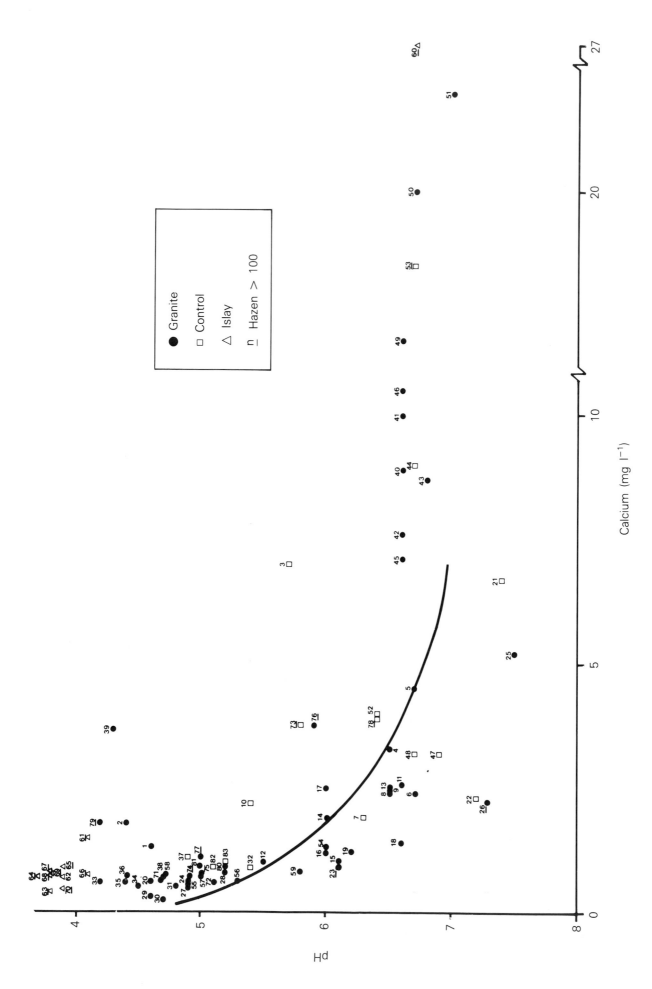

Figure 4. The distribution of pH and calcium values from all the sites studied. The values are the means from outflow samples. The curve is that of Henriksen (1979) but not all the sites are applicable because of their alkalinity or organic content.

that any general conclusions concerning the chemistry must be drawn with care. However, the close relationship which exists in the chemistry of most pairs (Figure 2), which were almost always collected at least 24 and sometimes as much as 72 hours apart, suggests that the data are meaningful for these waters, at least during the period of sampling. In addition, extensive data of this kind have been rare in the past (Watt Committee on Energy 1984; United Kingdom Acid Waters Review Group 1986) and should be explored when available.

The water sample taken from the outflow of each loch was assumed to be representative of the chemistry of that loch at that time. This was not necessarily true of the sample from the main inflow, whose chemistry bore a variable relationship with that of the outflow depending on local conditions. At most sites, the chemistry of the outflow and the main inflow was similar (Figure 3). However, there are a number of exceptions which are of considerable interest, where one or more of the chemical determinands differed substantially in the inflow and outflow waters. A good example of this difference was at Loch Grannoch in Galloway in May 1984, where the pH of the inflow was 6.2 whereas that of the outflow was 4.6. Smaller differences were noted at subsequent visits, but it is evident that inflows of this type may be very signi-ficant in allowing the survival of brown trout in a system which is elsewhere lethal to them. Arctic charr, which are now extinct in Loch Grannoch, would not have entered these streams and would have been confined entirely to the loch.

The area of Scotland most affected by acidification appears to be Galloway in the south-west. Only here was a considerable proportion of the lochs chemically acidified, and this coincided with a loss of fish populations in many of them. In the same area at present, there are attempts to restore 2 of these systems chemically—Loch Dee (Burns et al. 1984) and Loch Fleet (Central Electricity Generating Board 1985). Judging by experience in Scandinavia (Henriksen 1982), these projects are likely to be successful in the short term, but expensive. A small number of lochs in other parts of Scotland are also affected by acidification (Plate 4).

These results reflect the experience in several other parts of the northern hemisphere (Drablos & Tollan 1980; Overrein et al. 1980; Haines 1981; Harvey & Lee 1982; Johnson 1982; Howells 1983) and agree with data produced by other workers in Scotland (Wright & Henriksen 1980; Harriman & Morrison 1980, 1981, 1982). However, a feature of the fresh waters in Scotland which seems to distinguish them, to some

Plate 4. Loch a Mhill Bhig near Loch Sloy in Strathclyde. Four small lochs close together were sampled in this area; 2 were on the granite block and contained no fish, whilst 2 adjacent 'control' lochs off the granite (Loch a Mhill Bhig being one of them) had normal populations of brown trout (Photograph K H Morris)

extent, from many of those in other geographic areas is the large proportion which have high organic staining. This factor needs to be emphasized more (cf Harriman & Wells 1985) and should be the subject of future research

5 References

Almer, B. 1974. Effects of acidification on Swedish lakes. *Ambio*, **3**, 30-36.

Anderson, M.P. & Bowser, C.J. 1986. The role of groundwater in delaying lake acidification. *Wat. Resour. Res.*, **22**, 1101-1108.

Battarbee, R.W. 1984. Diatom analysis and the acidification of lakes. *Phil. Trans. R. Soc. B*, **305**, 193-219.

Bjarnborg, B. 1983. Dilution and acidification effects during the spring flood of four Swedish mountain brooks. *Hydrobiologia*, **101**, 19-26.

Bobee, B. & Lachance, M. 1984. Multivariate analysis of parameters related to lake acidification in Quebec. *Wat. Resour. Bull.*, **20**, 545-556.

Brown, D.J.A. 1982. The effect of pH and calcium on fish and fisheries. *Water Air Soil Pollut.*, **18**, 343-351.

Brown, D J A. & Sadler, K. 1981. The chemistry and fishery status of acid lakes in Norway and their relationship to European sulphur emissions. *J. appl. Ecol.*, **18**, 433-431.

Burns, J.C., Coy, J.S., Tervet, D.J., Harriman, R., Morrison, B.R.S. & Quine, C P. 1984. The Loch Dee Project: a study of the ecological effects of acid precipitation and forest management on an upland catchment in south-west Scotland. 1. Preliminary investigations. *Fish. Manage.*, **15**, 145-167.

Cape, J.N., Fowler, D., Kinnaird, J.W., Paterson, I.S., Leith, I.D. & Nicholson, I.A. 1984. Chemical composition of rainfall and wet deposition over northern Britain. *Atmos. Environ.*, **18**, 1921-1932.

Central Electricity Generating Board. 1985. *The Loch Fleet Project.* London: Central Electricity Generating Board.

Drablos, D. & Tollan, A. 1980. *Ecological impact of acid precipitation.* (SNSF Project 72/80.). Oslo: SNSF.

Flower, R. & Battarbee, R.W. 1983. Diatom evidence for the recent acidification of two Scottish lochs. *Nature, Lond.*, **305**, 130-133.

Haines, T.A. 1981. Acidic precipitation and its consequences for aquatic ecosystems: a review. *Trans. Am. Fish. Soc.*, **110**, 169-707.

Harriman, R. & Morrison, B.R.S. 1980. Ecology of acid streams draining forested and non-forested catchments in Scotland. In: *Ecological impact of acid precipitation*, edited by D. Drablos & A. Tollan, 312-313. Oslo: SNSF.

Harriman, R. & Morrison, B.R.S. 1981. Forestry, fisheries and acid rain in Scotland. *Scott. For.*, **35**, 89-95.

Harriman, R. & Morrison, B.R.S. 1982. Ecology of streams draining forested and non-forested catchments in an area of central Scotland subject to acid precipitation. *Hydrobiologia*, **88**, 251-263.

Harriman, R. & Wells, D.E. 1985. Causes and effects of surface water acidification in Scotland. *Wat. Pollut. Contr.*, **84**, 215-224.

Harvey, H.H. & Lee, C. 1982. Historical fisheries changes related to surface water pH changes in Canada. In: *Acid rain/fisheries*, edited by R. E. Johnson, 227-242. New York: Cornell University.

Henriksen, A. 1979. A simple approach for identifying and measuring acidification of freshwater. *Nature, Lond.*, **278**, 542-545.

Henriksen, A. 1982. Susceptibility of surface waters to acidification. In: *Acid rain/fisheries*, edited by R. E. Johnson, 103-107. New York: Cornell University.

Howells, G.O. 1983. Fishery status and water quality in areas affected by acid deposition. *Water Sci. Technol.*, **15**, 67-80.

Johnson, R.E. 1982. *Acid rain/fisheries. Proc. int. Symp. on Acidic Rain and Fishery Impacts on Northeastern North America.* New York: Cornell University.

Overrein, L.N., Seip, H.M. & Tollan, A. 1980. *Acid precipitation—effects on forests and fish.* (SNSF Project 72/80.) Oslo: SNSF.

United Kingdom Acid Waters Review Group. 1986. *Acidity in United Kingdom fresh waters.* London: Department of the Environment.

Vangenechten, J.H.D. 1980. Interrelations between pH and other physico-chemical factors in surface waters of the Campine of Antwerp, (Belgium) : with special reference to acid moorland pools. *Arch. Hydrobiol.*, **90**, 265-283.

Watt Committee on Energy. 1984. *Acid rain.* London: Watt Committee on Energy.

Wright, R.F., Conroy, N., Dickson, W., Harriman, R., Henriksen, A. & Schofield, C.L. 1980. Acidified lake districts of the world. In: *Ecological impact of acid precipitation*, edited by D. Drablos & A. Tollan, 377-379. Oslo: SNSF.

Wright, R.F. & Henriksen, A. 1980. *Regional survey of lakes and streams in southwestern Scotland, April 1979.* (SNSF Project 72/80.) Oslo: SNSF.

Appendix 3

The status of fish populations in some lochs vulnerable to acid deposition in Scotland

R N B CAMPBELL

Summary

As part of a general survey of Scottish lochs on granite bedrock that had the aim of determining whether the acidification of lochs on granites in Galloway was occurring elsewhere, 83 lochs in granite areas throughout the country were visited. At 60 of these sites, fish samples were taken from the lochs (and usually also their associated streams), as were chemical samples and measurements of bathymetry. Data from lochs with appropriate chemistry were plotted on to Henriksen's (1979) acidification curve, from which it was seen that 17 could be classified as acidified. Various characteristics of brown trout populations from lochs falling above and below this curve were then compared, and it was found that these populations differed significantly in ways that could be attributed to reduced recruitment caused by the effects of acid rain on nursery streams.

1 Introduction

Lochs vulnerable to acidification are those oligotrophic waters with little or no buffering capacity. Those with little such capacity can be acidified temporarily by some acid episode; those with no capacity can be permanently acidified (Henriksen 1979). The effect of acidification on salmonid populations in such lochs is, however, mainly through damage to juvenile populations in the associated spawning burns (Harvey & Lee 1981). Reduced recruitment lowers the number of adults in the population, and there is a tendency for individual size to increase as more food becomes available for each individual (Harvey & Lee 1981; Haines 1981; Hay 1984) and the population as a whole ages. If recruitment fails entirely, then extinction eventually occurs.

Such characteristic effects of acidification on salmonid populations have been observed frequently in acidified waters in both Scandinavia and North America (Overrein *et al.* 1980) and have been regarded by some authors as useful indicators of the occurrence of acidification (Harvey 1975). In assessing the status of salmonid populations in lochs vulnerable to acidification in Scotland, therefore, these are the features that would indicate the advent or occurrence of such acidification.

For various reasons, including the fact that some of the first indications of the occurrence of acidification in Scotland were observed in lochs on granite in Gallo-

way (Wright & Henriksen 1980; Flower & Battarbee 1983), the other granite areas of the country were considered to be where the most significant damage might be occurring. From geological maps, therefore, a list was drawn up of all lochs over one ha in area with outflows, on granite bedrock. Groups of these lochs were selected from different parts of the country and a control, non-granite bedrock, loch chosen near to each group. These groups were then visited during 1984 and 1985.

2 Methods

Netting for adult fish was carried out in a total of 60 lochs during the study (Plates 1 & 2). The nets used were standard monofilament multi-mesh nylon gill nets, the panels of different mesh sizes (12 dimensions from 19-120 mm) being randomly ordered along the length. The intention was to net each loch in as standard a way as possible, one net set at the surface in open water, another set on the bottom on the littoral running out from the shore. However, the variety of lochs sampled meant that it was not always possible to maintain this standard. Some lochs had huge populations of small fish, so that only one net could be used if excessive catches were to be avoided. Large lochs, however, required more than a single net for realistic sampling. Other lochs were shallower than the depth of the nets (2 m) so that the distinction between surface and bottom setting disappeared. In a few cases, owners set quotas not to be exceeded and, in these cases, the nets were patrolled in daytime until the limit was reached.

Nettings that produced no fish were considered of particular interest if there was historical evidence of there having been natural populations in such lochs in the past. In an attempt to acquire such records, the list of potential survey lochs (and control lochs) was distributed to anglers in the hope that at least presence/absence information could be obtained. However, of the 400 or so questionnaires distributed, only about 20 were returned. This lack of response meant that 7 lochs which were found to be fishless had to be excluded from some analyses, it being uncertain if they had ever had a self-sustaining fish population.

At each loch visited, water samples were taken at the first visit and the last, from the major inflow and the outflow. The chemical analyses of these included pH,

Plate 1. Setting a gill net from a small inflatable boat in Loch Brandy in the Grampian Highlands (Photograph A A Lyle)

Plate 2. Lifting a gill net from the shore at Loch Pityoulish in Strathspey, one of the 'control' lochs sampled during this study (Photograph A A Lyle)

Hazen (to give an indication of organic content), aluminium and calcium. These analyses are discussed in detail elsewhere (Appendix 2).

All fish caught were identified and measured (fork and total length) to the nearest 5 mm. Each was weighed to the nearest 5 gm, sexed and a sample of scales was removed. Each fish was examined for external deformities. The largest 10 in each sample had samples of flesh removed for heavy metal analyses, and up to 30 in each sample had their stomach contents noted. Identification of the food items was to Order or Family and percentage occurrence (Hynes 1950) calculated for each category in each sample. The ecological groupings of prey taxa into bottom, mid-water, surface and zooplankton categories (Frost & Brown 1967) were also used.

3 Results

Although the lochs selected for this survey (apart from the controls) were on granite bedrock, not all proved to be low alkalinity, acid waters (Plate 3), so that a further selection was needed to focus on those actually vulnerable to acidification and where fish populations might be showing symptoms of damage (Table 1). Lochs that were alkaline and had calcium concentrations greater than 7 mg l^{-1} were excluded. The remaining clear water (Hazen<100) lochs with relevant netting data were plotted on Henriksen's (1979) acidification curve (Figure 1). This curve is based on the disruption that acidification causes to the natural proportions of calcium, bicarbonate and hydrogen ions in pristine, oligotrophic clear waters. As extra hydrogen ions enter the loch, bicarbonate is used up and acidity increases, leaving the calcium at a higher level

Table 1. Checklist of lochs fished during the survey.

Number	Loch name	Vulnerable	Fish	Status
1	Grannoch	A	T	G
2	Fleet	A	O	G
3	Lochenbreck	A	T	C
4	am Fhaing	B	T	G
5	nan Craobh	B	T	G
6	Tearnait	B	T	G
7	Dubha 'Morvern'	B	T	C
8	Caol	B	T	G
9	Uisge	B	T	G
10	Mhic Pheadair Ruadh	B	T	C
11	Dubh 'Kingshouse W'	B	T	G
12	Dubh 'Kingshouse N'	A	T	G
13	Dubh 'Kingshouse F'	B	T	G
14	Mathair Eite	B	T	G
15	Gaineamhach	B	T	G
16	Gaineamhach 'NE'	B	T	G
17	Gaineamhach 'SE'	B	T	G
18	Einich	B	T	G*
19	Beanaidh	B	T	G
20	Mhic Ghille-chaoil	A	T	G
21	Pityoulish	E	F	C
22	na Seilge	E	T	C
23	Talaheel	B	T	G
24	nan Clach Geala	A	O	G
25	Dubh Cul Na Beinne	E	T	G
26	Tuim Ghlais	E	T	G
27	Long L of the Dungeon	A	T	G
28	Round L of the Dungeon	A	T	G
29	Enoch	A	O	G*
30	Arron	A	O	G
31	Neldricken	A	O	G*
32	Dungeon	A	T	C
33	Narroch	A	O	G
34	Round L of Glenhead	A	T	G
35	Long L of Glenhead	A	T	G
36	Valley	A	O	G
37	Harrow	A	T	C
38	Dow	A	—	G
39	Dalbeattie Plantain	A	O	G
40	Fern	E	F	G
41	White	E	F	G*
42	Barean	E	F	G
43	Clonyard	E	F	G
44	Fellcroft	E	T	C
45	Bengairn	E	T	G
46	Duff's	E	T	G
47	Kernsary	E	T	C
48	Ghiuragarstidh	B	T	C
49	Policies	E	O	G
50	Waterton	E	T	G
51	of Skene	E	T	G*
52	Brandy	A	T	C
53	Corby	E	T	C
54	Muick	B	T	G*
55	Dubh 'Muick'	A	T	G
56	Buidhe	B	T	G
57	Lochnagar	A	—	G
58	nan Eun	A	O	G
59	Sandy	B	T	G
60	Bharradail	E	T	C
61	Beinn Uraraidh	E	T	C
62	nam Breac	A	T	C
63	nam Manaichean	E	O	C
64	Laoim	E	—	C
65	Sholum	E	—	C
66	Sholum 'W'	E	—	C
67	Leorin 'W'	E	—	C
68	Leorin 'E'	E	—	C
69	na Beinne Brice	E	—	C
70	'Moine na Surdaig'	E	—	C
71	Coirre Fhionn	A	—	G
72	Iorsa	A	T	G
73	Garbad	E	T	C
74	Cnoc an Loch	E	T	G
75	a'Mhuillin	A	T	G
76	Kirkaldy	E	T	G
77	a'Chaoruinn	E	T	G
78	an t'Sidhein	E	T	C
79	nan Stuirteag	E	T	G
80	a'Mhill Bhig	A	T	C
81	a'Mhill Bhig 'Lower'	A	T	C
82	Maol Meadhonach 'Upper'	A	O	G
83	Maol Meadhonach 'Lower'	A	O	G

A = above Henriksen curve
B = below Henriksen curve
E = excluded
T = trout present
F = no trout, but other fish present
O = no fish present
— = no information on fish available (usually = not fished)
G = granite (G* = fringe group)
C = control

Plate 3. Bengairn Loch in Galloway, though lying entirely on granite making up the Criffell block, is not acidified (probably due to adequate buffering material in the drift) (Photograph P S Maitland)

than normal and thus marking out acidified from acid waters.

This principle does not apply to brown waters containing high concentrations of natural organic acids and which are specifically excluded from use with this acidification curve (Henriksen 1979). The position of these brown waters relative to acidification is uncertain as they do not appear to be common in Scandinavia or North America where most acidification research has taken place. Figure 1 also shows a generalized relationship between pH and calcium made for Scottish lochs by Holden (1956). Seventeen different lochs appear above the curve (though there are 18 points, as Loch Grannoch was sampled in both April and December 1984) and are to be considered as acidified on this criterion; 16 appear below the curve as unacidified— though acidifiable.

The aim of the analysis was to determine if this acidification curve, based on Norwegian chemical criteria, separated lochs with fish populations damaged in the manner described above from undamaged ones. The first comparisons made between the 2 groups of lochs, those above and below the curve, were for non-biological differences—altitude and time of sampling (number of days from the 1st January to the sampling date). Neither proved significant (Mann-Whitney U-test values were 97 and 125 respectively

for $n1=18$ and $n2=16$). There were no significant altitudinal or temporal differences between the 2 groups of lochs, and therefore no evidence that any differences could be attributable to other causes.

The average relative fish density, average individual size and condition factor of fish from the 2 groups of lochs all proved to be significantly different (Table 2).

There was no significant difference in average fish age between the 2 groups (Figure 2), which was surprising given the difference in average size. The implication of this finding may be that the fish in the acidified group were larger for their age than those in the unacidified group, and this implication is confirmed in Figure 3. The former group was significantly larger on average in the I+ age class ($U=6$ for $n1=5$ and $n2=9$), the II+ ($U=22$ for $n1=11$ and $n2=14$) and the III+ ($U=27.5$ for $n1=11$ and $n2=14$), but there was no significant difference between the older age classes. The more rapid growth to a similar size plateau in the acidified growth suggests that they were reaching the mature size faster and, as the values in Figure 3 show, in the II+ and III+ classes there were more mature fish in this group—though the differences are not significant.

These differences are all explicable by reduced recruitment giving more resources to those surviving, as shown in Figure 4: in 62% of the streams associated

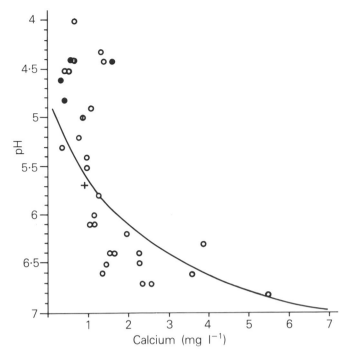

Figure 1. A plot of all non-peaty (Hazen <100) lochs for which valid netting results were obtained, on the Henriksen (1979) acidification curve. Zero catches from lochs for which no historic record of natural populations could be found were regarded as invalid. Halved circles represent lochs with identical co-ordinates. Filled circles or semi-circles show lochs in which no fish were netted but for which there is historic evidence of natural populations in the past. The + is a generalized value for Scottish lochs of the pH to be expected at a calcium concentration of 1 mg l^{-1} (Holden 1956)

with the acidified lochs, no juvenile fish were recorded, compared to only 18% of the streams in the other group (cf Harriman & Morrison 1980, 1981, 1982) (Plates 4 & 5).

There is also evidence from the analyses of diet that fish in the acidified group have better feeding, as the average percentage occurrence of benthic food is significantly greater in their diets, while surface food and zooplankton are more common in the other group (Table 3). The only significant qualitative difference within the ecological groupings of diet organisms was in the greater occurrence of Sphaeriidae in the diet of the unacidified group (U=24).

4 Discussion

The results of this study show that brown trout populations in Scottish lochs identifiable as acidified on Norwegian chemical criteria (Henriksen 1979) have population characteristics (reduced numbers, increased individual size and condition, faster growth and possibly earlier maturity) consistent with reduced recruitment and consequent increase in individual resources. This attribution is given independent support by the absence of juvenile fish from over half the nursery streams associated with such lochs that were examined. Although only 5 acidified lochs, all in one small area of Galloway, have lost fish populations altogether, these results show that trout populations in another 6 lochs in that area are affected, and that a further 6 lochs in other parts of Scotland show the same traits. However, 16 lochs apparently also vulnerable to acidification throughout the country did not show these population traits, suggesting localized phenomena.

The results are broadly in agreement with studies of fish populations in acidified waters elsewhere (Muniz & Leivestad 1980; Howells 1983). Reduced numbers in both salmonid and non-salmonid populations affected by acidification have been widely recorded in Norway (Wright & Snekvic 1978; Rosseland et al. 1980) and in North America (Harvey & Lee 1981). In an interesting study by Ryan and Harvey (1977), a link was made between increased individual growth rate in rock bass (*Ambloplites rupestris*), reduced population density and environmental stress.

The effect of reduced population density in increasing fish size has been noted for pike (*Esox lucius*) and

Table 2. Summary of the differences between brown trout populations of lochs above and below Henriksen's (1979) acidification curve

Parameter	Group average		Mann-Whitney U-test statistic
	Above	Below	
Population density (fish/net/night)	4.71	15.03	44*
Population density excluding zero catches	6.39	15.03	44*
Average fish size (fork length mm)	225	181	35*
Condition of fish (K factor)	1.29	1.19	33*

* The significance level for n1=18 and n2=16 is 86 and applies to the first population size test. All other tests do not include the 5 lochs with no fish, and their significance level is 59 for n1=13 and n2=16

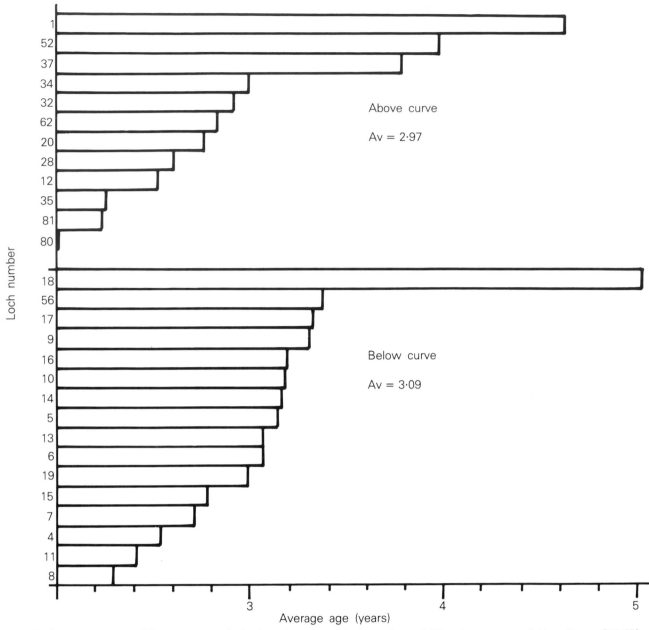

Figure 2. Average ages of brown trout in lochs above and below the acidification curve of Henriksen (1979)

perch (*Perca fluviatilis*) in Sweden (Almer 1974), brown trout in Scotland (Hay 1984) and for a wide variety of salmonids and non-salmonids in North America (Harvey 1975). Such reduced population density does not inevitably improve growth. Rosseland *et al.* (1980) found no such general response in sparsely populated lakes in Norway, despite the significantly fuller stomachs of fish there, and postulated that there is some energy cost in living in acid water. Harvey and Lee (1981) also found that there was no constant relationship between growth and population density in acidified waters in North America; it depended on the local effects of metabolic stress, population density and food supply. In a study of yellow perch (*Perca flavescens*) in acidified waters in Canada, Ryan and Harvey (1980) found increased growth in the more acid waters until their third year, after which it became slower, corresponding to a change in diet from invertebrates to fish. Improvement in the individual

condition of fish in acidified waters has been recorded for brown trout by Rosseland *et al.* (1980) in Norway and for some populations of a variety of species in North America by Harvey (1975).

The effect of acidification on the age structure of a fish population shows a similar pattern of a general or classical response, ie an ageing structure, with a number of deviations. In North America, Harvey and Lee (1981) report ageing of populations of yellow perch in acidified waters, but the contrary for some white sucker (*Catostomus commersoni*) populations—the loss of age classes over 3 years old. In Scandinavia, Rosseland *et al.* (1980) report a similar situation for both brown trout and perch: in general, ageing populations but with examples of the contrary (populations with no older fish at all), suggesting that in such cases the effort of spawning is fatal. In this study, the average age of fish from acidified waters did not prove

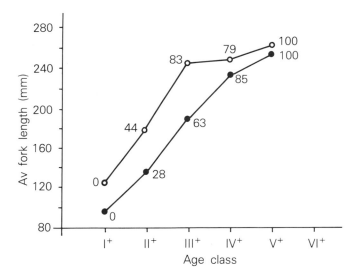

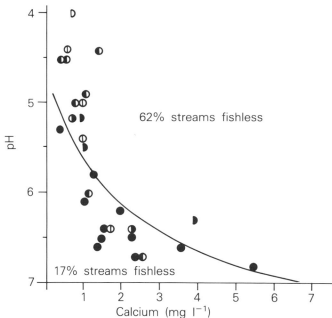

Figure 3. Average size of age classes of brown trout from lochs above and below the acidification curve of Henriksen (1979). Filled circles are populations below the curve, numbers are the percentage of mature fish in each age class

Figure 4. Presence (●) or absence (○) of juvenile brown trout in inflows (left semi-circle) and outflows (right semi-circle) associated with lochs containing adult fish. Percentages refer to groups above and below Henriksen's (1979) acidification curve

to be any greater than that from unacidified, although their average size was greater, and it was shown that the fish grew significantly faster until their fourth year.

In fact, a population that fails only gradually will retain a fairly normal age structure, though with reduced numbers. Only if recruitment ceases abruptly and completely will an ageing and abnormal age structure be produced. The former may be the more common situation in Scotland, where spring snowmelt is of less significance than in either Scandinavia or North America. In both these regions, poisoned spring snowmelt can wipe out eggs and young regularly each year, causing an abrupt end to recruitment. The variable, usually milder, winters in Scotland are less likely to have such a dramatic effect. It could be, however, that the larger size of the fish in acidified lochs makes them more susceptible to netting or brings them into the lochs earlier than their smaller contemporaries in unacidified systems can enter their more crowded lochs. Another explanation for this result would be that of Frenette and Dodson (1984), who found differential mortality of the smaller fish in each age class of brook charr (*Salvelinus fontinalis*) in acidified lakes in Canada.

The perturbations in normal calcium metabolism in spawning white suckers (Beamish *et al.* 1975) suggest

extra stress at spawning for fish in acidified waters of the sort that could explain the examples that have no post-spawners. There is evidence of the inhibition or delay of spawning in such waters for white suckers (Beamish *et al.* 1975), roach (*Rutilus rutilus*) (Bengtsson *et al.* 1980), fathead minnows (*Pimephales promelas*) (Mount 1983), and perch (Rask 1984). If spawning occurs, there is evidence of reduced survival of eggs and fry in many species. Brown (1982) showed that the most sensitive time for brown trout was immediately after fertilization but that survivability improved with age. Similar findings have been made for Sunapee charr (*Salvelinus arcticus*) (Jagoe *et al.* 1984), brook charr (Gunn & Keller 1984) and Pacific salmon. Reduced recruitment, therefore, can be caused by mortality at any stage of spawning or juvenile growth.

Although there have been a number of reports of increased growth and improved condition from populations of fish in acidified waters, there has never been a report of the logical corollary to such effects, earlier maturity. As a general rule, the better growth enjoyed

Table 3. Average percentage occurrence of taxa in the diets of brown trout populations in lochs above and below Henriksen's (1979) acidification curve

Ecological category	Group average		Mann-Whitney U-test statistic
	Above	Below	
Bottom foods	56	24	38.5*
Mid-water foods	28	28	95
Surface foods	23	32	60.5
Zooplankton	3	11	60.5

* The significance level at 95% is 58 for n1=17 and n2=16

Plate 4. A typical gill net sample from an acidified loch, Loch Grannoch in Galloway, taken in May 1984. This loch lies entirely on granite and is acidified according to the chemical criteria of Henriksen (1979). As the photograph shows, there is a lack of young fish (average age 4.6 years). Fish here are scarce (average 1.6 per net night), but are large (average 276 mm) and in good condition (average K factor 1.29) (Photograph R N B Campbell)

by salmonids, the quicker they mature (Alm 1959), and whether they mature depends on reaching a certain minimum size by a certain time of year. So, if growth is accelerated, maturity is reached earlier (Frost & Brown 1967). A natural consequence of increased size and condition through reduced numbers would, therefore, be earlier maturity. The figures for proportion matured per age class found in this study, although not statistically significant between the acidified and non-acidified groups, are suggestive and, given the plausibility of such an effect, deserve consideration.

The dietary evidence from this study, showing improved nutrition of fish in acidified waters, supports the conclusion of reduced density derived from the population parameters. In such lochs, there would be a larger area of benthic food-producing littoral zone per fish and less need for the fish to feed on surface or mid-water prey, as is suggested by the results. This conclusion is in contrast to the situation reported elsewhere, where the improved condition of fish in acidified waters is related to the increase in such mid-water animals as corixids (Kelso *et al.* 1982; Overrein *et al.* 1980). There was no evidence of a general increase in feeding on corixids in this study, though some fish from Loch Grannoch fed very heavily on them.

The impression gained of the state of brown trout populations in acidified lochs in Scotland is that the process of acidification has been mild and gradual, and is still continuing. There does not seem to have been a sharp cut-off in recruitment leaving a population to age and die out, but rather a gradual reduction of numbers of all ages, with consequent increasing individual growth and condition factor of those remaining.

It may be that, as discussed above, in Scotland the spring snowmelt is so much less than in Scandinavia and North America that the effects of accumulated winter acidity on spawning streams is much less dramatic (cf Bjarnborg 1983; Henriksen *et al.* 1984). It should also be noted that it is probably during winter that the peat content of runoff from the Scottish uplands is at its highest. If so, then the increased aluminium toxicity to be expected with decreased pH in snowmelt would not occur in Scotland as it does elsewhere (though see Vangenechten 1980). It certainly seems possible that much of Scotland, however base-poor the bedrock, could be organically buffered against the worst forms of aluminium toxicity by the overlying peat.

The general conclusion from this study is that acidification damage to fish populations does occur in Scot-

Plate 5. A typical gill net sample from an acid loch, Loch Tearnait in Morvern, Argyll, taken in June 1984. This loch lies entirely on granite but is not acidified (Henriksen 1979). As the photograph shows, there is no lack of young fish (average age 2.9 years). Fish here are more numerous (average 6.5 per net night) but are smaller (average 197 mm) and not in such good condition (average K factor 1.12) as in the acidified Loch Grannoch (Plate 3) (Photograph R N B Campbell)

land, though at present severe damage is confined mainly to Galloway (Plate 6). It is apparent, too, that in some lochs that still have fish populations there are signs of stress attributable to recruitment failure likely to have been caused by acidification within nursery streams. Possibly many of such populations may become extinct in the next decade.

5 References

Alm, G. 1959. Connection between maturity, size and ages in fishes. *A. Rep. Inst. Freshwat. Res. Drottningholm.,* no. **40,** 5-145.

Almer, B. 1974. Effects of acidification on Swedish lakes. *Ambio,* **3,** 30-36.

Beamish, R.J., Lockhart, W.L., Van Loon, J.C. & Harvey, H.H. 1975. Long term acidification of a lake and resulting effects on fishes. *Ambio,* **4,** 98-102.

Bengtsson, B., Dickson, W. & Wyberg, P. 1980. Liming acid lakes in Sweden. *Ambio,* **9,** 34-36.

Bjarnborg, B. 1983. Dilution and acidification effects during the spring flood of four Swedish mountain brooks. *Hydrobiologia,* **101,** 19-26.

Brown, D.J.A. 1982. The effect of pH and calcium on fish and fisheries. *Water Air Soil Pollut.,* **18,** 343-351.

Drablos, D. & Tollan, A. 1980. *Ecological impact of acid precipitation.* (SNSF Project 72/80.) Oslo: SNSF.

Flower, R. & Battarbee, R.W. 1983. Diatom evidence for the recent acidification of two Scottish lochs. *Nature, Lond.,* **305,** 130-133.

Frenette, J.J. & Dodson, J.J. 1984. Brook trout (*Salvelinus fontinalis*) population structure in acidified Lac Tawtare. *Can. J. Fish. aquat. Sci.,* **41,** 865-877.

Frost, W.E. & Brown, M.E. 1967. *The trout.* London: Collins.

Gunn, J.M. & Keller, W. 1984. Spawning site water chemistry and lake trout *(Salvelinus namaycush)* sac fry survivability to spring snowmelt. *Can. J Fish. aquat. Sci.,* **41,** 319-329.

Haines, T.A. 1981. Acidic precipitation and its consequences for aquatic ecosystems: a review. *Trans. Am. Fish. Soc.,* **110,** 669-707.

Harriman, R. & Morrison, B.R.S. 1980. Ecology of acid streams draining forested and non-forested catchments in Scotland. In: *Ecological impact of acid precipitation,* edited by D. Drablos & A. Tollan, 312-313. Oslo: SNSF.

Harriman, R. & Morrison, B.R.S. 1981. Forestry, fisheries and acid rain in Scotland. *Scott. For.,* **35,** 89-95.

Harriman, R. & Morrison, B.R.S. 1982. Ecology of streams draining forested and non-forested catchments in an area of central Scotland subject to acid precipitation. *Hydrobiologia,* **88,** 251-263.

Harvey, H.H. 1975. Fish populations in a large group of acid stressed lakes. *Verh. int. verein. theor. angew. Limnol.,* **19,** 2405-2417.

Plate 6. Loch Neldricken in Galloway once held populations of brown trout and of pike. Like several other lochs in the same area (eg Lochs Enoch and Valley) which lie entirely on granite, it is now acidified and fishless (Photograph R N B Campbell)

Harvey, H.H. & Lee, C. 1981. Historical fisheries changes related to surface water pH changes in Canada. In: *Acid rain/fisheries*, edited by R. E. Johnson, 227-242. New York: Cornell University.

Hay, D. 1984. Acid rain—the prospect for Scotland. *Proc. A. Study Course., Inst. Fish. Manage.,* **15,** 110-118.

Henriksen, A. 1979. A simple approach for identifying and measuring acidification of fresh water. *Nature, Lond.,* **278,** 542-545.

Henriksen, A., Skogheim, O.K. & Rosseland, B.O. 1984. Episodic changes in pH and aluminium-speciation kill fish in a Norwegian salmon river. *Vatten,* **40,** 255-260.

Holden, A.V. 1956. Fertilization experiments in Scottish freshwater lochs. II. Sutherland, 1954. 1. Chemical and botanical observations. *Scient. Invest. Freshwat. Salm. Fish. Res.,* **24,** 1-42.

Howells, G.O. 1983. Fishery status and water quality in areas affected by acid deposition. *Water Sci. Technol.,* **15,** 67-80.

Hynes, H.B.N. 1950. The food of fresh-water sticklebacks (*Gasterosteus aculeatus* and *Pygosteus pungitius*), with a review of methods used in studies of the food of fishes. *J. Anim. Ecol.,* **19,** 36-58.

Jagoe, C.H., Haines, T.A. & Kircheis, F.W. 1984. Effect of reduced pH on three life stages of Sunapee char *Salvelinus alpinus. Bull. environ. Contam. Toxicol.,* **33,** 430-438.

Johnson, R.E. 1982 *Acid rain/fisheries. Proc. int. Symp. on Acidic Rain and Fishery Impacts on Northeastern North America.* New York: Cornell University.

Kelso, J.R.M., Love, R.J., Lipsit, J.H. & Dermott, R. 1982. Chemical and biological status of headwater lakes in the Sault Ste Marie District, Ontario. In: *Acid precipitation; effects on ecological systems*, edited by F. M. D'Itri, 165-208. Ann Arbor: Ann Arbor Science.

Mount, D.I. 1983. Chronic effect of low pH on fathead minnow survival, growth and reproduction. *Wat. Res.,* **7,** 987-993.

Muniz, I.P. & Leivestad, H. 1980. Acidification—effects on freshwater fish. In: *Ecological impact of acid precipitation*, edited by D. Drablos & A. Tollan, 84-92. Oslo: SNSF.

Overrein, L.N., Seip, H.M. & Tollan, A. 1980. *Acid precipitation—effects on forests and fish.* (SNSF Project 72/80.) Oslo: SNSF.

Rask, M. 1984. The effect of low pH on perch (*Perca fluviatilis* L.) III: the perch population in a small acidic, extremely humic forest lake. *Annls zool. fenn.,* **21,** 15-22.

Rosseland, B.O., Sevaldrud, I.H., Svalastog, D. & Muniz, I.P. 1980. Studies on freshwater fish populations—effects of acidification on reproduction, population structure, growth and food selection. In: *Ecological impact of acid precipitation*, edited by D. Drablos & A. Tollan, 336-337. Oslo: SNSF.

Ryan, P.M. & Harvey, H.H. 1977. Growth of rock bass (*Ambloplites rupestris*) in relation to the morphoedaphic index as an indicator of an environmental stress. *J. Fish. Res. Bd Can.,* **34,** 2079-2088.

Vangenechten, J.H.D. 1980. Interrelations between pH and other physico-chemical factors in surface waters of the Campine of Antwerp, (Belgium): with special reference to acid moorland pools. *Arch. Hydrobiol.,* **90,** 265-283.

Wright, R.F. & Henriksen, A. 1980. *Regional survey of lakes and streams in southwestern Scotland, April 1979.* (SNSF Project 72/80.) Oslo: SNSF.

Wright, R.F. & Snekvic, E. 1978. Acid precipitation—chemistry and fish populations in 700 lakes in southernmost Norway. *Verh. int. verein. theor. angew. Limnol.,* **20,** 765-775.

Appendix 4

The status of fish in streams associated with lochs vulnerable to acid deposition in Scotland

P S MAITLAND

Summary
Fish in the inflow and outflow streams of 63 Scottish lochs were sampled by electro-fishing; 50 of these lochs had granite catchments, whereas the catchments of the other 13 'control' lochs were of other types of bedrock. Seven species of fish were found in the streams concerned, but only one of these—brown trout (*Salmo trutta*)—was common. Some 33% of the loch inflows and 32% of the outflows were apparently fishless. The majority of these sites were shown to be acidified according to the acidification curve of Henriksen (1979). Many of the other granite sites and virtually all the 'control' sites had fish in the streams (usually in both inflow and outflow). In most cases, several year classes were present—although 0+ fish always dominated. Most of the streams where the absence of fish appeared to be associated with acidification occur in south-west Scotland.

1 Introduction
Following the evidence from Scandinavia and North America of extinctions of fish populations in numerous acidified lakes (Almer 1974; Harvey 1975; Wright & Snekvic 1978; Overrein *et al.* 1980; Haines 1981; Harvey & Lee 1982; Johnson 1982; Muniz & Leivestad 1982; Schofield 1982), considerable concern has been expressed about the status of fish in Scottish lochs and streams in relation to the known high levels of acid deposition here (United Kingdom Review Group on Acid Rain 1983; Cape *et al.* 1984; Watt Committee on Energy 1984).

The dominant fish in the majority of these lochs is the brown trout (*Salmo trutta*), and special attention was given to this species during this study. Because it has an ecological requirement for running water, both for spawning and for nursery grounds, the populations of fish in the inflowing and outflowing streams of the lochs selected for study were examined wherever possible. Such streams are known to be vulnerable to acid pulses under certain weather conditions (Bjarnborg 1983).

Attention within the project has been centred on lochs whose basins and catchments lie on granite bedrock— much of the current evidence suggests that these are likely to be the most vulnerable sites to acidic deposition from the atmosphere. From a comprehensive study of the 1:50000 OS maps and equivalent geological maps, it was possible to identify all the granite lochs in Scotland. Groups of these granite lochs in different parts of the country were chosen for field study and, in addition, a nearby 'control' loch (whose catchment lies on non-granitic rocks) was selected for each group. Only lochs which had at least one associated stream shown on the map were included in the study.

2 Methods
Eighty-three lochs were visited during 1984 and 1985. At each loch, the major inflowing stream and the outflow were sampled for fish by means of a portable back-pack electric fishing machine ('Safari 100' Electro Fisher). This machine was normally used to fish upstream from a suitable point for a standard period of time, and the length and width of the stream so sampled were noted (Plate 1). All fish caught were identified, measured for length and returned to the stream alive. Fishing time was kept relatively short (usually 10–20 minutes) in order to minimize use of electricity, because some sites were over 10 km uphill from the nearest vehicle access and all equipment had to be carried there.

For a variety of reasons, it was not possible to sample streams at all 83 loch sites. Several had no permanent inflow large enough to hold fish, a few had no outflow, or both were completely silted or dried up (Plate 2). Fishing conditions were variable and occasionally difficult due to bad light, high flows, overhanging vegetation, etc, and the data cannot be regarded as quantitative.

3 Results
3.1 General
Of the 83 sites involved in the study, it was possible to obtain data on the fish in 58 inflowing streams and 63 outflowing ones. Only 4 sites had no inflow or outflow of any kind, and at several others the small size of the stream (from which, however, water samples could be taken) or its nature (restricted access for fish, siltation, etc) virtually precluded fish surviving there.

3.2 Species
A list of species collected during the entire study (Table 1) shows that 3 of the total of 10 involved (arctic charr, roach and perch) were never found in streams. Of the others, Atlantic salmon, pike and nine-spined stickleback were uncommon. By far the most widespread fish were brown trout (64.5% of the sites

Plate 1. Sampling for trout and other small fish in the outflow from Loch Gaineamhach on the Moor of Rannoch (Photograph K H Morris)

studied). Eels (22.6%), three-spined stickleback (12.9%) and minnows (4.8%) were less common, but occasionally abundant. Eleven (17.8%) of the sites fished apparently had no fish of any kind present in either the inflow or the outflow.

3.3 Fish communities

Nineteen (33%) of the loch inflows which were studied apparently contained no fish. Of the others, 29 (50%) contained brown trout only, 8 (14%) brown trout and at least one other species, and 2 (3%) contained no brown trout but at least one other species.

Twenty (32%) of the loch outflows apparently contained no fish. Of the others, 17 (27%) contained brown trout only, 14 (22%) brown trout and at least one other species, and 12 (19%) no brown trout but at least one other species.

3.4 Site characteristics

The distribution of the pH and calcium values of the waters studied in relation to the curve of Henriksen (1979) indicates that many of them appear to be acidified (Figures 1 & 2). Of the 19 fishless inflows found, 17 (89%) lie above the curve and only 2 (11%) below it. Similarly, with the 20 fishless outflows, 17 (85%) lie above the curve and only 3 (15%) below it. The absence of fish in these streams, therefore, may well be associated with the acidified conditions there.

Table 1. Summary of all data on fish species from inflows to and outflows from loch sites

Fish species	Number of sites	% total sites
Atlantic salmon (*Salmo salar*)	1	1.6
Brown trout (*Salmo trutta*)	40	64.5
Arctic charr (*Salvelinus alpinus*)	0	0
Pike (*Esox lucius*)	1	1.6
Minnow (*Phoxinus phoxinus*)	3	4.8
Roach (*Rutilus rutilus*)	0	0
Eel (*Anguilla anguilla*)	14	22.6
Three-spined stickleback (*Gasterosteus aculeatus*)	8	12.9
Nine-spined stickleback (*Pungitius pungitius*)	1	1.6
Perch (*Perca fluviatilis*)	0	0
Sites with no fish	11	17.8

56

Plate 2. The dried up outflow from Loch Beanaidh in Strathspey. At sites like this it was not possible to fish or to take water samples from either inflow or outflow during dry weather (Photograph A A Lyle)

brown trout only, 14 (22%) brown trout and at least one other species, and 12 (19%) no brown trout but at least one other species.

3.4 Site characteristics

The distribution of the pH and calcium values of the waters studied in relation to the curve of Henriksen (1979) indicates that many of them appear to be acidified (Figures 1 & 2). Of the 19 fishless inflows found, 17 (89%) lie above the curve and only 2 (11%) below it. Similarly, with the 20 fishless outflows, 17 (85%) lie above the curve and only 3 (15%) below it. The absence of fish in these streams, therefore, may well be associated with the acidified conditions there.

Of the 10 fishless lochs for which inflow and outflow fish data are available, it should be noted that fish were found in 3 of the streams involved. However, in all 3 of these cases the fish concerned were eels which occurred only in the outflows. No fish were ever found in the inflows of these fishless lochs and trout were always absent from associated streams. The pH and calcium characteristics of almost all these sites are low (Figures 1 & 2).

The majority of the sites studied (Table 2) had fish in the loch and in its associated pair of streams. Chemical conditions were apparently acceptable in these situations and in only 3 (6%) of the streams was the pH below 5.0. In those situations where fish were absent from an inflow or an outflow, conditions were usually poorer and the pH was below 5.0 in 6 (23%) of them (Figure 3).

A particularly interesting situation was found at Loch Grannoch in Galloway. This large loch once maintained an important sport fishery for brown trout and one of the few populations of arctic charr in south-west Scotland. Over the last 3 decades the fishery has deteriorated and virtually ceased, and arctic charr have apparently become extinct. Much of the catchment of the loch has been afforested over this period. There are still some brown trout in the system, however, and it appears that they are being maintained by recruitment from the main inflow stream, where young fish were found on several occasions during this study and whose pH is normally around 6.0. In contrast, the outflow (which must reflect much of the chemistry of the loch) is fishless and acid, often with a pH below 5.0. Unfortunately, the catchment of the main inflowing stream has itself recently been afforested and it seems likely that this will follow the fate of the rest of the system and brown trout will disappear completely.

3.5 Stream populations

As indicated above, the data on the numbers of fish in streams were obtained in a standard way but were not really quantitative. When standardized, the numbers of trout found in a standard area of stream bear little relation to the numbers of adults found in standard netting in the loch (Figure 4), although most lochs with trout did have young in the inflow or outflow or both.

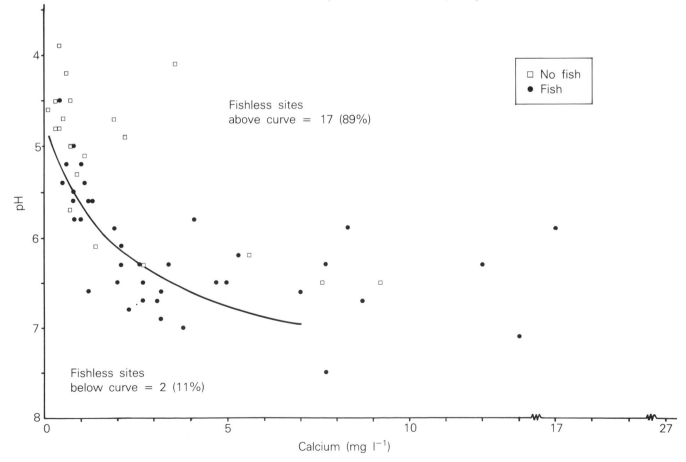

Figure 1. The distribution of pH and calcium plots for all inflow streams fished during this study

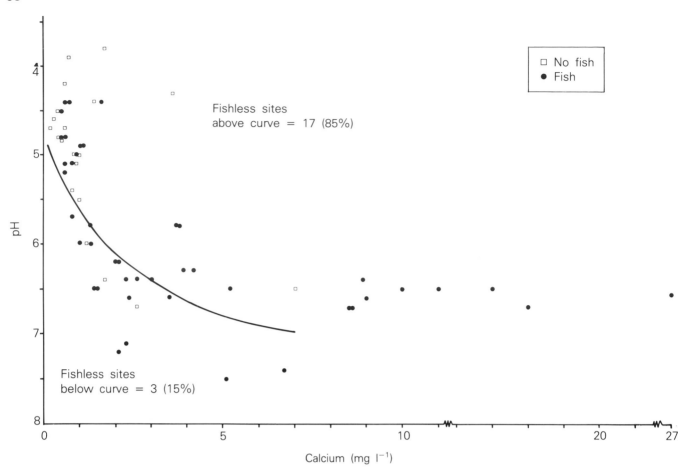

Figure 2. The distribution of pH and calcium plots for all outflow streams fished during this study

Table 2. The numbers of young trout in each 0.5 cm length group at the sites investigated during the study. Some sites (—) were not fished

Loch number	0		1		2		3		4		5		6		7		8		9		10		11+
1	—	—	—	—	1	2	1	3	7	—	—	—	—	—	—	—	1	1	2	1	3	1	2
2	—	—	—	—	—	—	—	—	—	—	—	—	—	—	—	—	—	—	—	—	—	—	—
3	—	—	—	—	10	36	8	10	—	—	—	1	—	—	—	—	1	1	1	2	—	—	1
4	—	—	—	—	—	2	8	3	—	—	—	—	—	—	—	—	1	—	—	—	—	1	—
5	—	—	—	—	—	—	1	2	1	—	—	2	—	1	3	2	—	—	—	1	1	1
6	—	—	—	—	—	—	4	1	1	2	—	2	—	—	—	1	1	—	—	—	—	—	1
7	—	—	—	—	—	1	1	1	—	—	—	2	—	—	—	—	1	2	—	—	—	—	—
8	—	—	—	—	—	—	—	—	—	—	—	—	—	—	—	—	—	—	—	—	—	—	—
9	—	—	—	—	—	—	—	—	—	—	2	—	—	—	—	1	1	—	1	2	—	1	1
10	—	—	—	—	—	—	3	13	8	2	—	—	—	—	1	—	1	—	—	—	—	1	1
11	—	—	—	—	—	—	—	—	—	—	—	—	—	—	—	—	1	1	—	1	—	1	1
12	—	—	—	—	—	—	—	—	—	—	—	—	—	—	—	—	—	—	—	—	—	—	—
13	—	—	—	—	—	—	—	—	—	—	—	—	—	—	—	—	1	—	—	—	—	—	3
14	—	—	—	—	—	—	—	6	20	8	—	—	2	—	2	4	3	—	1	1	2	—	2
15	—	—	—	—	—	—	1	6	7	3	5	1	—	—	—	—	2	1	—	—	—	—	—
16	—	—	—	—	—	—	1	4	—	—	—	—	—	—	—	—	—	—	—	—	—	—	—
17	—	—	—	—	—	—	2	13	25	6	2	—	—	—	—	—	1	1	1	—	—	—	—
18	—	—	—	—	—	—	1	3	2	—	—	—	—	—	3	—	—	—	—	—	—	—	2
19																							
20	—	—	—	—	—	—	—	—	2	1	1	—	—	—	—	1	2	—	—	—	—	—	—
21	—	—	—	—	—	—	—	—	—	—	—	—	—	—	—	—	—	—	—	—	—	—	—
22	—	—	—	—	—	—	1	3	9	13	6	5	3	1	—	—	1	—	3	—	1	—
23	—	—	—	—	—	—	—	—	—	—	—	—	—	—	—	—	—	—	—	—	—	—	—
24	—	—	—	—	—	—	—	—	—	—	—	—	—	—	—	—	—	—	—	—	—	—	—
25	—	—	—	—	—	—	—	—	—	—	—	4	4	1	—	—	—	—	—	—	—	—
26	—	—	—	—	—	—	1	2	1	1	1	2	4	—	—	—	—	—	—	—	1	—	—
27	—	—	—	—	—	—	—	—	—	—	—	1	4	1	—	—	—	—	—	—	—	1	2
28	—	—	—	—	—	—	—	—	—	—	—	—	—	—	1	2	—	—	—	—	4	—	1
29	—	—	—	—	—	—	—	—	—	—	—	—	—	—	—	—	—	—	—	—	—	—	—
30	—	—	—	—	—	—	—	—	—	—	—	—	—	—	—	—	—	—	—	—	—	—	—
31	—	—	—	—	—	—	—	—	—	—	—	—	—	—	—	—	—	—	—	—	—	—	—

32	—	—	—	—	—	—	—	—	—	—	—	—	—	—	—	—	—	—	—	—	—	—
33	—	—	—	—	—	—	—	—	—	—	—	—	—	—	—	—	—	—	—	—	—	—
34	—	—	—	—	—	—	—	—	—	—	—	—	—	—	—	—	—	—	—	—	—	—
35	—	—	—	—	—	—	—	—	—	—	—	—	—	—	—	—	—	—	—	—	—	—
36	—	—	—	—	—	—	—	—	—	—	—	—	—	—	—	—	—	—	—	—	—	—
37	—	—	—	—	—	—	—	—	—	—	—	—	—	—	—	—	—	—	—	—	—	—
38																						
39	—	—	—	—	—	—	—	—	—	—	—	—	—	—	—	—	—	—	—	—	—	—
40	—	—	—	—	6	10	7	—	—	—	—	—	—	1	1	1	1	—	1	—	—	1
41	—	—	—	—	—	—	—	—	—	—	—	—	—	—	—	—	—	—	—	—	—	—
42	—	—	—	—	—	—	—	—	—	—	—	—	—	—	—	—	—	—	—	—	—	—
43	—	—	—	—	—	—	—	—	—	—	—	—	—	—	—	—	—	—	—	—	—	—
44	—	—	—	—	—	1	9	7	1	—	1	2	—	—	—	—	—	—	—	—	—	—
45	—	—	—	—	1	14	10	7	2	—	—	—	—	—	—	—	—	—	—	—	—	—
46	—	—	—	—	—	—	—	—	—	—	—	—	—	—	—	—	—	—	—	—	—	—
47																						
48																						
49	—	—	—	—	—	—	—	1	—	2	2	3	—	—	—	—	—	—	1	—	—	—
50																						
51																						
52	—	—	—	—	—	—	—	—	—	—	—	—	—	—	—	—	1	—	—	—	—	6
53	—	—	—	—	—	—	—	—	—	—	—	—	—	—	—	—	—	—	—	—	—	2
54	—	—	—	—	—	1	2	2	—	1	3	1	—	—	2	—	—	—	—	1	2	—
55	—	—	—	—	—	—	—	—	—	—	—	1	1	1	—	—	—	—	—	—	—	—
56	—	—	—	—	—	—	—	—	—	—	—	1	2	—	1	—	1	2	—	—	—	—
57	—	—	—	—	1	1	—	—	—	—	—	—	—	—	—	—	—	—	—	—	—	—
58	—	—	—	—	—	—	—	—	—	—	—	—	—	—	—	—	—	—	—	—	—	—
59	—	—	—	—	—	2	—	—	—	—	—	—	—	1	2	1	—	—	—	—	—	1
60	—	—	—	—	—	—	—	—	—	—	—	—	1	—	—	—	—	—	—	—	—	—
61	—	—	—	—	—	—	—	—	—	—	—	—	—	—	—	—	—	—	—	—	—	—
62	—	—	—	—	—	—	—	—	—	—	—	—	—	—	—	—	—	—	—	—	—	—
63																						
64																						
65																						
66																						
67																						
68																						
69																						
70																						
71																						
72																						
73																						
74																						
75																						
76	—	—	—	—	—	1	—	—	—	3	3	2	—	1	—	1	—	—	—	1	—	1	3
77	—	—	—	—	—	—	—	—	—	2	—	2	—	—	—	—	—	—	—	—	—	—
78	—	—	—	—	—	—	—	—	—	3	1	3	1	—	—	—	—	—	—	—	—	2
79	—	—	—	—	—	—	—	—	—	—	—	—	—	—	—	—	—	—	—	—	—	—
80	—	—	—	—	—	—	—	—	—	1	—	—	—	—	—	—	—	—	1	—	—	—
81	—	—	—	—	—	—	—	—	—	—	—	—	—	—	—	—	—	—	—	—	—	1
82	—	—	—	—	—	—	—	—	—	—	—	—	—	—	—	—	—	—	—	—	—	—
83	—	—	—	—	—	—	—	—	—	—	—	—	—	—	—	—	—	—	—	—	—	—

Because of the differences in the years and seasons of sampling, the relative sizes of trout in the various streams are not of too great comparative significance. However, the size distribution within streams is of interest in relation to acidification and the suggestion that whole year clases can be removed by one acidic episode (Beamish *et al.* 1975; Frenette & Dodson 1984; Henriksen *et al.* 1984). As is normal in nursery streams, especially small ones, most streams were dominated by 0+ fish though other year classes were usually present too. However, only in a few places were older fish present in significant numbers.

Of the 63 sites where stream fish were sampled, 25 had no trout, 9 had one year class only, 9 had 2 year classes, 13 had 3 year classes and 7 had 4 year classes. The presence of year classes was estimated from an analysis of the length/frequency data available. The great majority of the sites with several year classes were between pH 5.5–7.0 and 1–10 mg l^{-1} calcium (see Brown & Sadler 1981; Brown 1982).

4 Discussion

The results lead to the conclusion that, as in some parts of Wales (Stoner *et al.* 1984), fishless conditions in a number of streams in Scotland are associated with acidification (Plate 3) and that the majority of such sites are found in south-west Scotland (cf Wright & Henriksen 1980). Fish data for lochs and at least one associated stream are available for 63 sites. Of this

Plate 3. The inflow burn to Loch Neldricken in Galloway was once probably an important spawning and nursery stream for the brown trout in this loch, which is now acidified and fishless (Photograph A A Lyle)

Plate 4. The inflow burn to Fellcroft Loch in Galloway, one of the 'control' lochs off the granite blocks. This burn is not acidified and is used by both brown trout and minnows from the loch as a spawning and nursery area (Photograph P S Maitland)

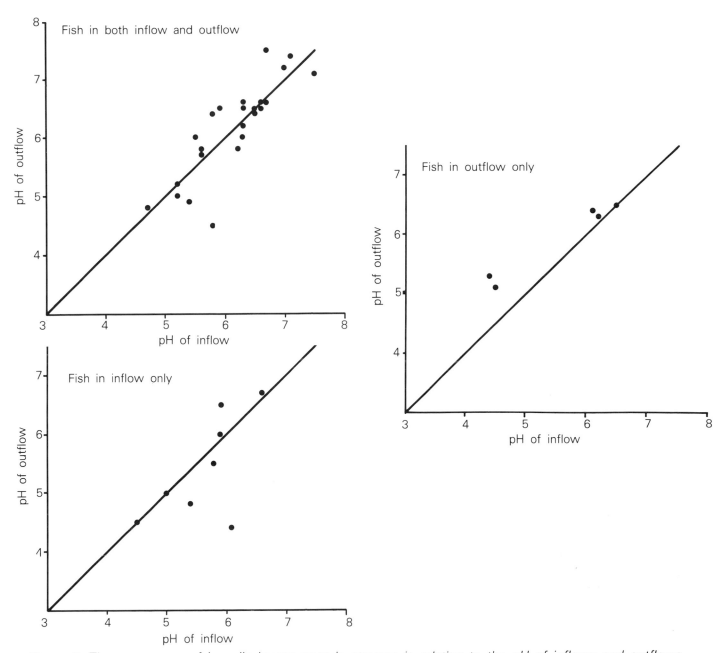

Figure 3. The occurrence of juvenile brown trout in streams in relation to the pH of inflows and outflows

number, 13 are 'control' sites (ie their catchments are not on granite bedrock but they are near sites whose catchments lie entirely on granite). All of these control sites have fish in the loch and usually at least one associated stream (Plate 4). In 3 cases (17%), fish were not found in streams associated with control sites.

Of the 48 lochs lying on granite and regarded as vulnerable, 7 have no fish in the loch or its streams, 3 of the lochs are fishless but have eels in the outflows, and one site has fish in the loch but none in the streams. Thus, 11 of the granite lochs (23%) have no trout in associated streams. Although some of these streams may have been infuenced by afforestation (Harriman & Morrison 1980, 1981, 1982), many had totally unafforested catchments.

As far as geography is concerned, the great majority of these fishless streams were found in south-west Scotland (cf Battarbee 1984), where a number of waters are known to be undergoing acidification (Burns *et al.* 1984). Only occasionally were fish absent from streams in other parts of the country.

Apart from systems from which fish have already disappeared, it is clear that some further extinctions are likely. Again, many of these will be in the Galloway area, and Loch Grannoch and perhaps the Lochs of Glenhead can be cited as examples. Thus, the next 2 decades are likely to see virtually all the lochs and streams on the granites of Doon and Cairnsmore fishless, unless conditions are alleviated. Even large lochs lying only partly on these granites may be in difficulty, and research by the author is in progress on Loch Doon, which contains the only known remaining population of arctic charr in south-west Scotland, to determine the status and likely future of this important system.

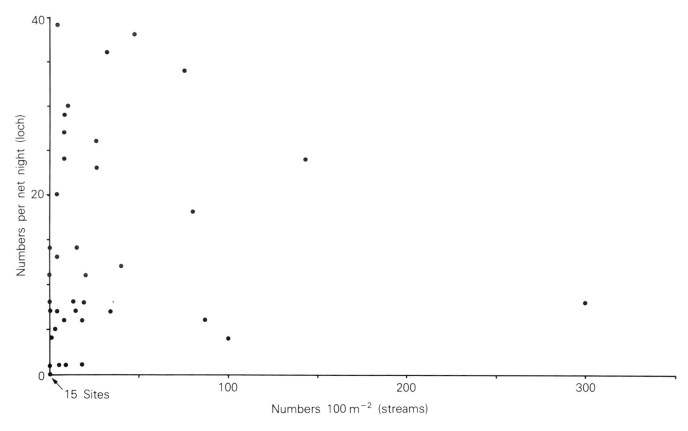

Figure 4. Plots of standardized catches of adult brown trout gill netted in lochs (numbers/net/night) and juvenile fish electric fished in the burns associated with each loch (mean values 100 m⁻² in inflow and outflow)

5 References

Almer, B. 1974. Effects of acidification on Swedish lakes. *Ambio, 3,* 30-36.

Battarbee, R.W. 1984. Diatom analysis and the acidification of lakes. *Phil. Trans. R. Soc. B,* **305,** 193-219.

Beamish, R.J., Lockhart, W.L., Van Loon, J.C. & Harvey, H.H. 1975. Long term acidification of a lake and resulting effects on fishes. *Ambio,* **4,** 98-102.

Bjarnborg, B. 1983. Dilution and acidification effects during the spring flood of four Swedish mountain brooks. *Hydrobiologia,* **101,** 19-26.

Brown, D.J.A. 1982. The effect of pH and calcium on fish and fisheries. *Water Air Soil Pollut.,* **18,** 343-351.

Brown, D.J.A. & Sadler, K. 1981. The chemistry and fishery status of acid lakes in Norway and their relationship to European sulphur emissions. *J. appl. Ecol.,* **18,** 433-431.

Burns, J.C., Coy, J.S. , Tervet, D.J., Harriman, R., Morrison, B.R.S. & Quine, C.P. 1984. The Loch Dee Project: a study of the ecological effects of acid precipitation and forest management on an upland catchment in south-west Scotland. 1. Preliminary investigations. *Fish. Manage.,* **15,** 145-167.

Cape, J.N., Fowler, D., Kinnaird, J.W., Paterson, I.S., Leith, I.D. & Nicholson, I.A. 1984. Chemical composition of rainfall and wet deposition over northern Britain. *Atmos. Environ.,* **18,** 1921-1932.

Frenette, J.J. & Dodson, J.J. 1984. Brook trout (*Salvelinus fontinalis*) population structure in acidified Lac Tawtare. *Can. J. Fish. aquat. Sci.,* **41,** 865-877.

Haines, T.A. 1981. Acidic precipitation and its consequences for aquatic ecosystems: a review. *Trans. Am. Fish. Soc.,* **110,** 669-707.

Harriman, R. & Morrison, B.R.S. 1980. Ecology of acid streams draining forested and non-forested catchments in Scotland. In:

Ecological impact of acid precipitation, edited by D. Drablos & A. Tollan, 312-313. Oslo: SNSF.

Harriman, R. & Morrison, B.R.S. 1981. Forestry, fisheries and acid rain in Scotland. *Scott. For.,* **35,** 89-95.

Harriman, R. & Morrison, B.R.S. 1982. Ecology of streams draining forested and non-forested catchments in an area of central Scotland subject to acid precipitation. *Hydrobiologia,* **88,** 251-263.

Harvey, H.H. 1975. Fish populations in a large group of acid stressed lakes. *Verh. int. verein. theor. angew. Limnol.,* **19,** 2405-2417.

Harvey, H.H. & Lee, C. 1982. Historical fisheries changes related to surface water pH changes in Canada. In: *Acid rain/fisheries,* edited by R. E. Johnson, 45-54. New York: Cornell University.

Henriksen, A. 1979. A simple approach for identifying and measuring acidification of freshwater. *Nature, Lond.,* **278,** 542-545.

Henriksen, A., Skogheim, O.K. & Rosseland, B.O. 1984. Episodic changes in pH and aluminium-speciation kill fish in a Norwegian salmon river. *Vatten,* **40,** 255-260.

Johnson, R.E. 1982. *Acid rain/fisheries. Proc. int. Symp. on Acidic Rain and Fishery Impacts on Northeastern North America.* New York: Cornell University.

Muniz, I.P. & Leivestad, H. 1980. Acidification—effects on freshwater fish. In: *Ecological impact of acid precipitation,* edited by D. Drablos & A. Tollan, 84-92. Oslo: SNSF.

Overrein, L.N., Seip, H.M. & Tollan, A. 1980. *Acid precipitation—effects on forests and fish.* (SNSF Project 72/80.) Oslo: SNSF.

Schofield, C.L. 1982. Historical fisheries changes in the United States related to decrease in surface water pH. In: *Acid rain/fisheries,* edited by R. E. Johnson, 57-59. New York: Cornell University.

Stoner, J.H., Gee, A.S. & Wade, K.R. 1984. The effects of acidification on the ecology of streams in the upper Tywi catchment in west Wales. *Environ. Pollut. A,* **35,** 125-157.

United Kingdom Review Group on Acid Rain. 1983. *Acid deposition in the United Kingdom.* Stevenage: Warren Spring Laboratory.

Watt Committee on Energy. 1984. *Acid rain.* London: Watt Committee on Energy.

Wright, R.F. & Henriksen, A. 1980. *Regional survey of lakes and streams in southwestern Scotland, April 1979.* (SNSF Project 72/80.) Oslo: SNSF.

Wright, R.F. & Snekvic, E. 1978. Acid precipitation—chemistry and fish populations in 700 lakes in southernmost Norway. *Verh. int. verein. theor. angew. Limnol.,* **20,** 765-775.

Appendix 5

Tail deformities in brown trout from acid and acidified lochs in Scotland

R N B CAMPBELL

Summary
Most old records of tail deformities in brown trout proved to be from lochs which are now acidified and fishless. Examination of trout from other lochs which are thought to be acidified but still have some trout revealed significant deformities in the tails of some of these fish too. The relevance of these findings to the acidification of Scottish lochs is discussed.

1 Introduction
In 1871, a 'tailless' brown trout (*Salmo trutta*) from the island of Islay in Scotland was exhibited at a meeting of the British Association for the Advancement of Science (Peach 1872). The caudal rays of this fish anastomosed towards the end, giving the tail a rounded appearance, hence the name (Plate 1). Similarly deformed trout were reported from Loch Enoch (Plate 2) in Galloway (Traquair 1882) and later from various streams in the central belt of Scotland (Traquair 1892). The identical nature of the deformity reported from both Islay and Galloway was noted by Traquair (1892), but at the time, though it was felt that the cause of the deformities was pollution, at least for those examples from industrial areas, this hypothesis could not explain the island and upland examples.

A further Galloway example was reported in 1927, from Loch Narroch, which is only 2 km from Loch Enoch (MacDonald 1927), and another from Loch Fleet in 1948 (Williams 1948). At present, Lochs Enoch, Narroch and Fleet are fishless (Maitland *et al.* 1986), and on the acidification curve of Henriksen (1979) are acidified. The question, therefore, arose as to whether these deformities were early indicators of acidification

Plate 1. One of the earliest tailless trout recorded. A specimen from Loch nam Maorachan (now called Loch nam Manaichean on Islay, which is held in the Royal Scottish Museum in Edinburgh. This loch is now fishless (Photograph Royal Museums of Scotland)

Plate 2. Loch Enoch in Galloway where tailless trout were recorded by Traquair in 1882. The fishing guide of this period stated that catches of 4–5 dozen trout were common at this time. The loch is now fishless (Photograph P S Maitland)

affecting the fish, either through increased acidity itself or associated aluminium toxicity.

The possible connection between fish deformities and acidification was not one of the original objectives of the programme to investigate the status of fish populations in Scottish lochs in relation to acidification (Maitland *et al.* 1986), although the story of the 'tailless trout' of Loch Enoch (already identified as acidified by previous researchers) was well known in Scottish limnology. The decision to investigate this particular topic was taken only after reference to similarly deformed trout having occurred in Loch Fleet (also identified as acidified) was found in unpublished angling records. Fortunately, this information was noted before the first fish caught during the Scottish survey were processed, so it was possible to examine them for deformities, even though they had been caught before this topic became part of the programme. As these deformities had also been reported from Islay (as well as Galloway), it was decided to include several lochs there in the survey, even though these lochs were not on granite bedrock, the original criterion for selection.

2 Methods
During the processing of brown trout caught during the survey, each was examined for deformities of the caudal fin rays. The descriptions used to define the typical deformity seen in the past were those of Traquair (1892), based on a thorough examination of fish from both Islay and Galloway. Essentially, the deformity of interest is a waviness and clumping of the fin rays of the dorsal and/or ventral edges of the caudal fin. Some of the fish recorded last century had such a strong degree of distortion that the whole tail had a rounded-off appearance, which gave rise to the names of 'tailless' or 'dock-tailed' trout. It is clear from the literature that these were exaggerated exceptions and that milder distortions of the caudal fin rays were commoner.

Drawings and dissections of the various types of deformity are shown in Traquair (1892). When deformed tails were found in the present study, they were first photographed on the whole fish and then removed and preserved. Some tails were also X-rayed at the Royal Museum of Scotland in Edinburgh, where some of the original specimens from Islay are still preserved. In most cases, the commonest type of deformity was a linear waviness in the rays, and a rounded appearance was found only in a few fish

3 Results
The present chemical nature of the lochs concerned has been discussed by Maitland *et al.* (1986).

3.1 General

Of 34 relevant lochs sampled in different parts of Scotland, 3 produced brown trout which had deformed tails: one loch was on Islay, the other 2 were in Galloway (Table 1). The lochs previously recorded as having such fish were all found to be fishless now—the loch on Islay that produced the first records of deformity has been included in Table 2 for interest, despite having a Hazen value of 100, which is at the limit set here for working with the acidification curve of Henriksen (1979).

All the lochs which produced deformed fish were acidified on the criterion of this acidification curve, as were all those lochs from which deformed trout had been reported in the past. No examples of the deformity were found in unacidified lochs. These results are summarized in Figure 1, which indicates that the number of fish caught per night decreases as lochs become more acid, and that, as catches become very small, both the number of lochs that have lost trout and the proportion of deformed fish increase.

3.2 Islay

Two lochs were netted here: Loch nam Manaichean (which was called Loch nam Maoachan when the deformed trout in it were originally reported) and Loch nam Breac, 0.5 km to the north and at a slightly lower altitude.

Loch nam Manaichean was found to be fishless. Peach (1872) reported that all trout caught in this loch over the previous 30 years had had deformed tails and that such fish were not found in any nearby loch, or indeed in any other loch on the island. Thompson (1872) stated that the nearby Loch nam Breac 'abounds in small trout having the usually formed homocercal caudal fins'. In August 1985, however, 10 out of the 13 brown trout caught in this loch had deformed tails, the nature of which is well seen on X-rays of the fins. The Hazen values for these lochs

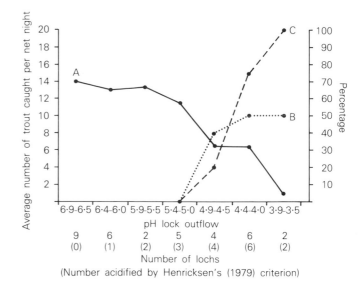

Figure 1. The relationship between loch acidity and: A, gill net catches of trout; B, the percentage of lochs with extinct populations; C, the percentage of deformed fish in the catches. NB The calculation of average catches per net night excluded zero catches from lochs with extinct populations

indicate that the surrounding peat is the probable source of their acidity.

Local information indicated that 2 other lochs on Islay, the Leorin Lochs, had lost trout populations known to have been present in the 1930s. These lochs were not netted during this study, but chemical samples indicated that they are very acidic (pH 3.8) and peat stained (Hazen>250).

3.3 Galloway

Loch Enoch and 7 neighbouring lochs were netted during the present survey. Loch Enoch had had a good reputation as a trout fishery last century, but by 1883 was regarded as having few fish and was only visited by anglers wishing to catch the 'tailless trout' for

Table 1. Lochs in which brown trout with deformed tails were found during this study

| Loch | Catch | | Date | Chemistry | |
	Deformed	Total	1985	pH	Hazen
Round Loch of Glenhead	1	1	May	3.7	15
Loch Harrow	2	10	May	4.7	5
Loch nam Breac	10	13	Aug	4.0	85

Table 2. Lochs from which brown trout with deformed tails have been recorded in the past

| Loch | Catch | Date | First reference to deformed fish | Chemistry | |
				pH	Hazen
Loch Enoch	0	Oct '84	Traquair 1882	4.6	5
Loch Narroch	0	May '85	MacDonald 1927	3.5	10
Loch Fleet	0	Apr '84	Williams 1948	4.4	20
Loch nam Manaichean	0	Aug '85	Peach 1872	3.9	100

which it had become famous (MacDonald 1927). The trout seem to have become extinct by 1890 at the latest, and when netted in October 1984 none were found. The nearest lochs, at a slightly lower altitude, Neldricken, Valley and Narroch, were also found to be fishless. In 1913, a trout with a deformed tail was caught in Loch Narroch, and in 1927 it was said of this loch '..the trout are becoming tailless and I hear have, within recent years, become so scarce that it is quite possible they may entirely disappear' (MacDonald 1927).

The Glenhead Lochs were netted in April 1985 and fish were found in both. The Round Loch of Glenhead yielded only one trout which had a deformed tail (Plate 3), but the Long Loch of Glenhead produced 11 trout and one minnow (*Phoxinus phoxinus*) none of which showed deformities. McDonald (1927) stated that he had fished the Round Loch of Glenhead many times and had caught many fish there, none of which were deformed. The lowest altitude lochs in this area that were netted, the Long and Round Lochs of the Dungeon, both produced trout in October 1984 and no records are known of there ever having been deformed fish in either of them. The histories and status of trout populations in these lochs are shown in Figure 2.

Loch Fleet was netted in April 1984 and found to be fishless. Angling records showed the trout here to have become extinct in the 1960s. Deformed fish, called 'half-tailed trout' were caught here in 1947 and 1948 (O Williams, unpublished angling diaries), and, interestingly, were described as being 'typically hard fighting half-tailed trout', which may indicate that the deformity is not too much of a disadvantage.

Loch Harrow does not lie on granite and was one of the 'control' lochs in this study. However, it is an acid loch and much of its catchment is now afforested. When netted in April 1985, 2 out of the 10 trout caught had deformed tails.

4 Discussion

After these deformities were reported, a number of theories were put forward as to the cause. The examples from industrialized areas were attributed to water pollution (Traquair 1892), but it was felt that this could not be the cause on an Hebridean island or in the upland areas of Galloway, where Loch Enoch was described as being '. . . away from every possible source of contamination . . .' (MacDonald 1927). Analyses were made of water from both Loch nam Manaichean and Loch Enoch and no pollutants were found, the very purity of the waters giving rise to a theory that the deformities were due to calcium deficiency and were, in fact, a form of 'rickets' (Traquair 1892). However, as was pointed out at the time, such an explanation would not account for the lowland polluted waters.

Other theories of mechanical damage or damage by other fish were easily refuted by examination of the deformed tails, which showed that the fin rays, though abnormal, were entire, unabraded and unbitten (Traquair 1892). The cause remained a mystery at the time, essentially because of the assumption that such island and upland lochs were beyond the reach of any form of pollution. In recent years, the discovery of just how far aerial pollution can travel has shown this assumption to be wrong, and the evidence from diatom cores is that Loch Enoch was beginning to acidify as early as the 1840s (Battarbee 1984). MacDo-

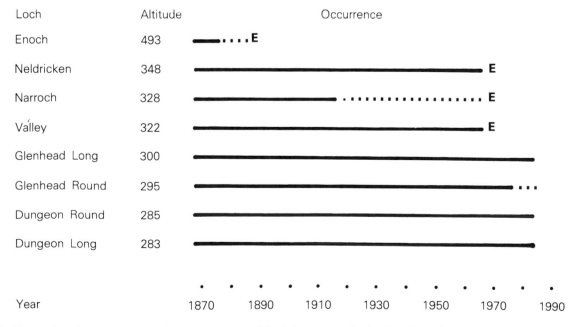

Figure 2. Records of appearance of brown trout with deformed tails (....) and their later extinction (E) in some lochs on the Doon granite block in Galloway. All dates are approximate

nald (1927) was prescient in being concerned at the 'public health' implications of the extinction of fish in such a remote place as Loch Enoch, but was unable to suggest any actual cause.

Deformities of fish due to water pollution are now well known in both fresh (Slooff 1982) and salt (Bengtsson 1985) water, and have now been particularly linked to acidification in North America, the sources of acidity being either mining operations (Mount 1973) or acid rain (Beamish et al. 1975; Fraser & Harvey 1982). It is not known whether the tail deformity apparently related to acidification in Scotland is produced during the egg or larval stages only, or whether it can be induced at any age whilst the fish is growing. Daye and Garside (1980) did hatch salmonid eggs at various acidities but did not rear any of the young concerned. Slooff (1982), working on bream (Abramis brama) in the polluted River Rhine, found that the most prevalent deformities, such as deformed fins, were most frequently seen in older fish.

In the Loch Enoch area, where there is a good altitudinal sequence of lochs identified as being acidified both by this study and others (Battarbee 1984), the fact that the occurrence of deformities precedes extinctions in relation to altitude is of interest. In Norway, the experience is that the effects

of acidification are first apparent in the highest hill lochs where catchments are small and soils are thin (Leivestad et al. 1976). The chronological and altitudinal sequence of deformities and extinctions in Scottish lochs agrees with this evidence (Figure 2).

On Islay, the loch which originally produced the deformed fish (Loch nam Manaichean) is the highest on the island, and the one from which fish were taken during this study (Plate 4) is only slightly lower. Even here, therefore, the sequence of the deformity suggests that aerial pollution rather than acidity from the surrounding peatland may be the cause.

Thus there is strong circumstantial evidence that, before populations of brown trout become extinct because of acidification, a characteristic deformity (Plate 5) of the caudal fin rays often appears. Direct proof can only be obtained through experimental rearing of fish in acidified waters, but the historical evidence in Scotland is that, every time that this deformity has been reported from a loch, it has been followed by the extinction of the fish population itself. The clear water lochs in which this sequence has occurred are all now identifiable as acidified on the criteria of Henriksen (1979). The situation on Islay is complicated by organic acidity in the lochs there, but the fact that the phenomenon occurred first in the

Plate 3. Brown trout with a deformed tail from the Round Loch of Glenhead in Galloway (April 1985). This loch is near several others which are now fishless. Earlier this century MacDonald (1927) stated that no deformed fish were known from this loch (Photograph R N B Campbell)

LOCH NAM BREAC, ISLAY
29.8.85

Plate 4. Tails of brown trout from Loch nam Breac on Islay, caught in August 1985. All but 3 have some deformity, but last century it was stated (Thompson 1872) that no deformed fish had ever been taken from this loch, whilst every year for 30 years most of the trout from the nearby Loch nam Maorachan had had deformed tails (Photograph R N B Campbell)

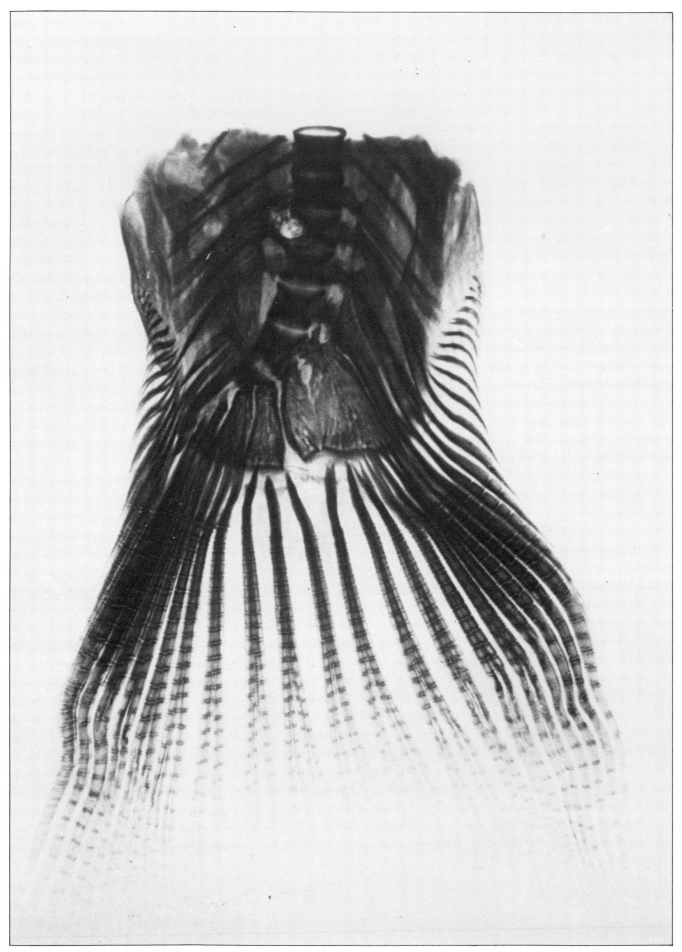

Plate 5. An X-ray of the deformed tail of a brown trout from Loch nam Breac on Islay (Number 12 in Plate 4) (Photograph Royal Museums of Scotland)

highest loch on the island, as it did first in the highest loch in Galloway, is suggestive of an air pollution effect.

These early deformed fish from Islay and Galloway may therefore have been the first ever indicators of man-made acidification of fresh waters in the British Isles, and the occurrence of similar deformities to-day may be a useful early sign of the process starting in other waters.

5 References

Battarbee, R.W. 1984. Diatom analysis and the acidification of lakes. *Phil. Trans. R. Soc. B*, **305**, 451-477.

Beamish, R.J., Lockhart, W.L., Van Loon, J.C. & Harvey, H.H. 1975. Long term acidification of a lake and resulting effects on fishes. *Ambio*, **4**, 98-102.

Bengtsson, B.E. 1985. Fish deformities and pollution in some Swedish waters. *Ambio*, **14**, 32-35.

Braekke, F. 1976. *Impact of acid precipitation on forest and freshwater ecosystems in Norway.* Oslo: SNSF.

Daye, P.G. & Garside, E.T. 1980. Structural alterations in embryos and alevins of the Atlantic salmon, *Salmo salar* L., induced by continuous or short-term exposure to acidic levels of pH. *Can. J. Zool.*, **58**, 27-43.

Fraser, G.A. & Harvey, H.H. 1982. Elemental composition of bone from white sucker (*Catostomus commersoni*) in relation to lake acidification. *Can. J. Fish. aquat. Sci.*, **39**, 1289-1296.

Henriksen, A. 1979. A simple approach for identifying and measuring acidification of fresh water. *Nature, Lond.*, **278**, 542-545.

Leivestad, H., Hendrey, G., Muniz, P.I. & Snekvic, E. 1976. Effects of acidic precipitation on freshwater organisms. In: *Impact of acid precipitations on forest and freshwater ecosystems in Norway*, edited by F. H. Braekke, 87-111. Oslo: SNSF.

MacDonald, J. 1927. The tailless trout of Loch Enoch. *Trans. Proc. Dumfries. Galloway nat. Hist. Antiq. Soc.*, **67**, 299-308.

Maitland, P.S., Lyle, A.A. & Campbell, R.N.B. 1986. *The status of fish populations in waters likely to have been affected by acid deposition in Scotland.* Natural Environment Research Council contract report to the Department of Environment and the Commission of the European Communities. Edinburgh: Institute of Terrestrial Ecology.

Mount, D.I. 1973. Chronic effect of low pH on fathead minnow survival, growth and reproduction. *Wat. Res.*, **7**, 987-993.

Peach, C.W. 1872. On the so-called tailless trout of Islay. *Rep. Br. Ass. Advmt Sci.*, **41**, 133-134.

Slooff, W. 1982. Skeletal anomalies in fish from polluted surface waters. *Aquat. Toxicol.*, **2**, 157-173.

Thomson, J. 1872. Peculiar trout of Loch Islay. *Sci. Gossip*, 1872, 85-86.

Traquair, R.H. 1882. On specimens of 'tailless' trout from Loch Enoch, in Kirkcudbrightshire. *Proc. R. phys. Soc. Edinb.*, **7**, 221-223.

Traquair, R.H. 1892. On malformed trout in Scottish waters. *Ann. Scot. nat. Hist.*, **1**, 94-103.

Williams, O. 1948. *Angling diary.* (Unpublished.)